HOW TO CATCH A DREAM

THERESA CHEUNG

HOW TO CATCH A DREAM

21 WAYS TO DREAM (AND LIVE) BIGGER AND BETTER

Thorsons

HarperThorsons
An imprint of HarperCollins*Publishers*
1 London Bridge Street
London SE1 9GF

www.harpercollins.co.uk

HarperCollins*Publishers*
1st Floor, Watermarque Building, Ringsend Road
Dublin 4, Ireland

First published by HarperThorsons 2022

1 3 5 7 9 10 8 6 4 2

A catalogue record of this book is
available from the British Library

ISBN 978-0-00-850198-3

Printed and bound in the UK using 100%
renewable electricity at CPI Group (UK) Ltd

MIX
Paper from
responsible sources
FSC™ C007454

This book is produced from independently certified FSC™ paper
to ensure responsible forest management.

For more information visit: www.harpercollins.co.uk/green

To all the big dreamers

Contents

WEEK THREE

Dream Catcher

SEVEN WAYS TO 'WAKE UP' IN YOUR DREAMS

'Is all that we see or seem
But a dream within a dream?'

Edgar Allan Poe

Behind your Eyes

You do not sleep. You believe you do because your body sleeps, but a deeply alert part of you never sleeps. While your body slumbers, *you* remain wide awake in the extraordinary world of your dreams.

As dreams rarely make sense, you may believe they are your brain simply reprocessing and consolidating the events and lessons of your waking life. But dreams are anything but meaningless. Not only are they the key to a more fulfilling life, but you can 'wake up' in them and gain truly life-changing insights with your eyes wide shut. If you use the twenty-one proven and practical nightly dreaming practices in this book, you will learn how to dream (and live) bigger and better.

BIGGER AND BETTER

'You mustn't be afraid to dream a little bigger, darling.' This delicious line from Eames, the character played by Tom Hardy in the science-fiction movie thriller *Inception* (2010), never fails to motivate me when my waking life feels diminished.

Inception marked a radical turning-point for me as an established dream-decoding author. It wasn't just because its mesmerizing cinematic depiction of the dream world made dreaming cool, everything about it ignited within me an intense desire to dream bigger and better myself.

From then onwards, I promised myself I would fully commit to better dream recall, deeper dream decoding and learning how to trigger the lucid dreaming state. And this book is the result of that commitment, and the techniques and approaches that actually worked for me. I've experienced first-hand their benefits for personal growth and seen how effective they can be for others. Today, I'm on a mission to bring dreams, in particular lucid ones, right out of the shadows, so they are no longer dismissed as nonsense or something to be feared. I want the whole world to catch their dreams and fall in love with them, and, by extension, themselves.

SO, WHAT IS A LUCID DREAM?

Dream recall and decoding is a potent self-help tool this book will explore but it will also introduce you to the art of lucid dreaming, which is the most vivid and creative way to dream. Lucid dreaming happens when the parts of your brain associated with cognitive functions, memory and self-awareness (the dorsolateral prefrontal cortex, the bilateral frontopolar prefrontal cortex, the praecuneus, the inferior parietal lobules and the supramarginal gyrus, to be precise!)[1] activate and you know you are dreaming *while* you are dreaming.

A lucid dream originates from a non-lucid dream.[2] In non-lucid dreams, the self-perception areas in the prefrontal cortex of your brain aren't as 'switched on', so you aren't aware you're dreaming. But when they are, and you become lucid, you become aware of your dream unfolding behind your very eyes. You can recognize thoughts and feel emotions. And sometimes you can change what you experience, which opens up infinite creative possibilities.

Common Myths about Lucid Dreaming

There's immense value in all dreaming. Recalling and decoding the messages of non-lucid dreams is hugely rewarding. It is also the clear path to lucid dreaming, which is often considered the Holy Grail of dream work. But sadly, there are common myths about lucid dreaming that may be muddying the waters or making you wary of experimenting with it.

'IT'S EXCEEDINGLY RARE.'

Becoming lucid while dreaming can happen to anyone. The experience is real.[3] Although we typically lack awareness when we dream, we all have the potential to become a remarkable exception. Lucid dreaming is more common in childhood, but is a learnable skill[4] that anyone can develop at any age.

'YOU CAN GET TRAPPED IN A LUCID DREAM.'

Dreams can feel long, but the longest that most last in real time is around fifteen to twenty minutes, so it is impossible to get stuck in a dream. For most people, managing to stay in a lucid dream is the real issue!

'YOU NEED TO BE SPIRITUAL TO LUCID DREAM.'

Although being mindful, imaginative and willing to think outside the box[5] increases the chances of lucidity, you don't need to meditate for hours, be an expert in esoteric yoga techniques, go on expensive spiritual retreats or take herbal cocktails to lucid dream.

'IT WILL CAUSE EXHAUSTION.'

Some people believe that you will wake up mentally tired or even depressed following a lucid dream because waking reality is a 'let down'. There is no evidence to suggest this. Lucid dreaming has a mood-boosting rather than draining impact. You wake up filled with a sense of excitement and appreciation of your hidden potential.

'SLEEP PARALYSIS IS NECESSARY FOR LUCID DREAMING.'

Sleep paralysis is when you wake up and your muscles are still asleep. It is associated with lucid dreaming and can be a precursor to it, but it isn't essential for lucid dreaming.

'IT'S SCARY.'

The first time you experience lucid dreaming it can feel disorientating, but the most commonly reported feelings are surprise and delight. If it does feel overwhelming, you can soon learn how to enjoy the experience. If the images are alarming, this has a lot to do with your waking state of mind filtering into your dreamscape. Use the inspiration of your ability to become lucid to create a more positive waking mindset.

'LUCID DREAMING IS CONTROLLING YOUR DREAMS.'

According to scientists,[6] lucid dreaming is a hybrid state of consciousness with elements of both sleeping and waking.

Contrary to what many people think, lucid dreaming isn't the ability to control your dreams. Thinking in terms of controlling your dreams will limit your ability to do so, as control is associated with domination. Instead, think of befriending your dreaming mind when you become lucid. In this gentle way you can influence some of what you want to experience in your dream, or you can choose to simply observe and let your dreaming mind 'surprise' you.

INSIDE OUT

Understanding yourself better and fulfilling your potential are what gives your life purpose and meaning. But in your waking hours, it's easy to get distracted. That's why your dreams matter. They remind you why you're breathing. They take you directly to the *heart* of things – what truly matters. They want you to know that your life isn't defined by the material, other people, your work or the external world, but by your *personal growth*. They shine a symbolic night light on things you haven't given enough attention to in your waking life and reveal what you are truly feeling about yourself, others and your life.

In essence, your dreams bring new perspectives and insights and the often neglected but invaluable power of deep and meaningful reflection into your life. They are messages from your heart which need to be reflected on but aren't, because in waking life thoughts from the head dominate. All of us could benefit from more reflection in our lives, and that's where the real power of dream work lies. Dreams encourage us to reflect.

Behind your sleeping eyes lies a whole new world of self-discovery, adventure and inspiration. You really can use your dreams to help you deal with difficult feelings, solve problems, boost your confidence and creativity, improve your relationships and teach yourself just about everything you need to know to live a more fulfilling life. The reason you haven't yet exploited their potential is probably because you don't believe you dream or because your dreams never make any sense. But be assured that you do dream. Everyone does. You just aren't recalling your dreams at the moment. And the reason they don't make sense is because they come from a different state of consciousness that speaks to you in a different language.

Fortunately, there are simple things you can do to boost your dream recall and decode the precious wisdom of your dreams. You'll find all these techniques outlined clearly and simply here. But more than that, what you learn will help you evolve into a *super dreamer* – someone who regularly becomes lucid and can use their dreams to transform their waking life.

HOW TO USE THIS BOOK

The format of this book lays the groundwork for a richer and more rewarding dream life. It starts with seven practices focusing on better dream recall, moves on to seven practices to trigger more vivid and creative dreaming, a practice dedicated to dream decoding wisdom followed by six radical practices for lucid dreaming. Every one of these twenty-one practices can increase your chances of lucid dreaming happening spontaneously, with the final seven most likely to induce it on a frequent basis.

Within these practices, I present different techniques for you to choose from, depending on what feels good to you.

You are strongly advised to take your time and learn one new technique each day. This shouldn't be a problem, as they are designed to fit into your routine effortlessly. At the end of each week, I provide a list of the practices and techniques so that you can tick off which seven you would like to try that week.

The first fifteen practices are for repeated daily use. Don't be tempted to skip them and jump straight to the final six practices. You may want to lucid dream right away, but good dream recall and a mindful approach to your waking reality are absolutely essential foundations for triggering lucidity. When your dream recall is established, you can perform the final six practices as and when.

Here's a snapshot of what lies ahead.

WEEK ONE: DREAM SEEKER

First things first. You can't tap into the infinite potential of your dreams if you don't recall them or enjoy recalling them. Not to mention that clear dream recall is the most crucial predictor of lucid dreaming. The seven practices introduced here, which you are advised to repeat daily, will help you recall your dream world.

WEEK TWO: DREAM DEEPER

Studies show that your dream world and your waking reality are interconnected. So the seven practices here encourage you to live your life intuitively, with a sense of curiosity, self-awareness and possibility that you can carry with you into your dreams. You'll also learn the optimum way to recall and record your dreams so that as week three begins you can effortlessly understand the secret picture language of your dreams and become your own dream decoder. Again, these practices are ones you are advised to repeat daily.

WEEK THREE: DREAM CATCHER

Yes, you really can learn how to 'wake up' in your dreams. Following the first practice, which offers basic dream decoding advice, the remaining six practices encourage more frequent episodes of lucid dreaming, helping you not only to awaken in your dreams, but potentially influence what happens in them. They build on the firm foundation of strong dream recall and awareness that the first two weeks aimed to establish, and with the exception of the first dream decoding practice, are not designed for daily but infrequent use.

THE DREAMS THAT MAY COME

As you work through the practices, expect more vibrant dreams to come to you at night and your waking life to feel richer as a result. You'll be on a new path to personal transformation in both your waking and your dream life.

Expect your self-awareness, emotional intellect and creativity to soar.[7] And as those night visions start lighting up your days and nights, remember catching your dreams is just the start. From now on you need to expect the unexpected, embrace change, get curious from the inside out and treasure every single dream as a precious gift, even those that cause confusion.

If you do have a dream that you simply can't make sense of and want a little extra help, feel free to get in touch. I'll do my best to reply in due course. One of the best things about being a dream author is reading *your* night visions. And I'd like to take this opportunity to invite you to prove to me how effective these twenty-one practices are for better dream recall, understanding and lucidity. You can find details of how to contact me on page 193, where, alongside suggested reading and recommended resources, you'll find a free gift exclusive to *How to Catch a Dream* readers and listeners.

CLOSE AND OPEN YOUR EYES

So, are you ready to begin a three-week voyage into your dreams and a happier waking life?

To begin, close your eyes briefly and commit silently to the twenty-one practices ahead. Think of them as your personal, nightly, inner GPS or nocturnal therapist, guiding you to ever wiser and more visionary versions of yourself. Then, open your eyes and turn the page. It's high time you start waking up each morning with truly astonishing dreams on your mind.

Dream Seeker

SEVEN WAYS TO 'SEE' YOUR DREAMS CLEARLY

'There are forgotten dreams stored in many layers. The deeper one digs, the closer they are. All fantastica rests on a foundation of broken dreams.'

Michael Ende

It's not yet known why dreams can often be hard to remember or to remember in their entirety rather than in fragments. Evidence suggests[1] that dream intensity and recall can decrease with age, but not as a rule. Some people find that their dreams become deeper and richer with age. What *is* known is that everyone dreams several times a night and people who find it easier to lucid dream are those who are able to recall their dreams on a regular basis.

It really is very simple: if you struggle to remember your non-lucid dreams, your chances of having a lucid dream are next to none. Clear and regular dream recall truly is the strongest indicator of whether or not you are going to have lucid dreams. It's also the most commonly neglected factor in dream work and not enough attention is paid to it by lucid dreaming experts, perhaps because it is so glaringly obvious.

That's why the first seven suggested practices are designed to significantly boost your chances of dream recall. All seven are designed to be repeated daily, and each has different options to choose from. The first practice offers a sound launching pad for bigger and better dreams. The second and third help you prepare for lift-off, while the final four are more practical in focus. Even if you don't typically have problems remembering your dreams, you'll still benefit hugely from trying out these seven dream-seeking suggestions. Not only will they help you remember your dreams with even greater frequency and clarity than before, but they will also help you establish the optimum creative, open-minded, relaxed mindset you need for lucid dreaming to occur spontaneously. Don't forget, too, that dream recall is healthy; it's a sign of emotional well-being.

Best of all, these seven practices will help you rediscover the joy – the natural high – of recalling the sense of possibility that clear dreaming can ignite in you. Without enjoyment and excitement sweeping you along like a current, your progress as a super dreamer is going to be seriously limited. So, aim to have as much fun as possible this week as you rediscover the joy of roaming in the weird and wonderful world of your dreams.

#1

Total Immersion

Whenever you dream, you experience an alternate reality, a fantastical world of your own creation. If you want to have dreams so creative and striking that you simply can't forget them on waking, it helps to immerse yourself in alternate realities that resemble the dream state as much as possible during the day, because your dreaming mind reflects and reacts to the stimuli you fuel it with.

Also, by immersing yourself totally in a creative, fantastical world when you are awake, you are 'practising' being and believing in an alternate reality, so when you start dreaming you feel totally at ease.

FIND YOUR WAY

GAME POWER

To my mind, there's no better dream-inducing stimulus than a thrilling video game. Now, if video gaming isn't for you, please don't toss this book aside, as I'll suggest some highly effective alternatives as well. But first I'm going to put video gaming centre stage to encourage you to give it a try. There is strong evidence[2] to suggest that video gamers are more likely to recall their dreams and have lucid dreams than non-video gamers.

It makes sense. Video games and dreams are both alternate realities. Of course, dreams come from your mind and video games from computers and consoles, but if you spend time gaming, you are typically immersed in a fictional, vibrant world; you are also aware it isn't real, with some control over what happens in it, just as you would be in a lucid dream. Both watching and influencing the action of a video-game character is suggestive of and good 'practice' for influencing your own lucid dream world.

In a game, you also have to master ways to overcome a series of threats to avoid elimination. The importance of facing, rather than running from threats in order to progress in a game can transfer into your dreams, reducing nightmares and also 'dream collapse', when the thrill of becoming lucid in a dream is so exciting it actually wakes you up (*see page* 155).

Game play makes it far more likely[3] that dream content will make its way into your mind. This is known as the 'Tetris effect',[4] which is when images or thoughts enter your mind, and dreams, after you perform an activity repeatedly. It comes from the video game Tetris.

Your emotional investment as you play is key. Whenever emotion appears in your waking life, your brain registers it as important and memorable, increasing the chances of you revisiting whatever scene or symbol ignited that emotion in order to understand it better. In addition, most games start off easy and then get more and more complicated to navigate to keep you constantly challenged and invested. Again, your dreaming mind wants a return on that energy investment when you fall asleep.

Another reason video games are more likely to enter your dreams is because of their shock value. If you don't give your waking mind enough suggestive symbolism and stimulation to feed the world of your dreams, your chances of having profound and memorable dreams decrease. That's why you tend to dream more when you go on vacation and your mind is kept busy with lots of new experiences to process. It's also why dreaming is more vivid if there's a lot of emotion and sudden change to process in your waking life. This is what happened during the pandemic lockdowns, when grief, fear and confusion surrounding Covid upended all our lives and people began to report a dramatic increase in vivid dreaming. It was dubbed 'the lockdown dream phenomenon'.

In a nutshell, video gaming is one of the simplest, safest and fastest ways to fuel your dreaming mind, so you are more likely to recall dreams that are magical rather than mundane. On top of all that, gaming can be fun, whatever age you are. And there is also its proven ability to improve your decision-making as well as mindful focus and concentration, which, as you'll learn later, are other crucial ingredients in your lucid dreaming tool-kit.

Find a Method That Suits You

Unless you are a seasoned gamer, your first challenge is to find a method of gaming that feels comfortable to you. (If you are, know that there is a certain type of game likely to boost dream recall and lucidity – *see page* 8.)

If you haven't gamed before, it can take a while to learn the ropes. But as with learning to ride a bike, once you get it, there's no stopping you.

There are a huge range of gaming options and you need to do some research to see what falls within your budget. Here are some options, in ascending price order:

- **SMARTPHONE GAMES:** You can find plenty of games to ignite your dreaming mind on the App Store or Google Play Store. There are also plenty of free gaming apps out there for you to test the waters with.

- **NINTENDO SWITCH LITE:** If you don't want to invest in high-end gaming, you can't go wrong with this portable option.

- **XBOX AND PLAYSTATION GAMES:** Both require an initial financial investment, and the technology of the consoles and the games themselves constantly require upgrading, but they have the advantage of being ready to go right out of the box.

- **VR (VIRTUAL REALITY) SIMULATOR GAMES:** Platforms such as Steam offer potent dream-inducing experiences if you are lucky enough to have a VR headset, the computer system requirements and the financial means.

Find the Game of your Dreams

The next challenge is to select a game that is going to significantly increase your chances of dream recall and lucidity. Any old game just will not do! It seems that the best type is one that is non-linear (one that doesn't follow a predetermined path and allows the player freedom of choice) and gives you plenty of options to roam freely in an open world, overcoming challenges to stay there.

Here are my top dream-igniting game suggestions:

- **SKYRIM (XBOX, NINTENDO SWITCH AND PLAYSTATION):** You can get lost in the best way possible in this fantastical setting complete with dragons, elves, orcs, magic, warring factions and adventure upon adventure. One of the game's great qualities – and why it is ideal for assisting lucid dreaming – is the uniqueness of the player's experiences. No two players experience the Skyrim world in the same way.

- **SHADOW OF THE COLOSSUS (PLAYSTATION):** This mysterious world, considered one of the finest video games ever created, is filled with rolling hills and a haziness that makes the whole experience feel just like you are wandering through a dream.

- **BATMAN ARKHAM ASYLUM (XBOX, PLAYSTATION):** The vulnerability you feel as the player is very reminiscent of a nightmare and if you can defeat the dark forces while playing as Batman, you can do it in your dreaming life.

- **NO MAN'S SKY (XBOX AND PLAYSTATION):** Offers 255 galaxies and 18 quintillion planets (yes, that's a real figure) for you to have the adventure of your dreams. Each planet contains unique procedurally generated biomes, animal life and landscapes. It would take you 585 billion years to visit every planet.

- **SKY: CHILDREN OF THE LIGHT (FREE MOBILE APP, NINTENDO SWITCH):** This is a massive open-world gaming experience in which to seek adventure.

Power Your Dreams

In 2019 the intimate connection between dreams, lucid dreaming and gaming came to life when Xbox Series X launched their fastest, most dynamic console to date: Power Your Dreams. A year later, dream scientists conducted lucid dreaming experiments that captured and decoded the dreams of gamers after they had experienced Xbox Series X. This then led to a dream content series called Made from Dreams that you may want to check out,[5] because it attempts to bring some of those lucid dreams to life in video form.

LOST IN WORDS

If you can't (or don't wish to) set aside thirty or so minutes a day for video gaming, then be sure to keep that time to lose yourself in a novel. (Indeed, you can double the impact of this total immersion technique by adding some gentle reading to your day *alongside* your gaming time.)

The dream-inducing reasons for reading fiction every day are similar to the reasons for gaming. When you read a great story or novel, you aren't being passive, as you would be if you watched a movie, where everything was imagined for you, but are busy visualizing what the narrative describes. In your mind's eye, you see how the characters and scenes look, sound and feel. You are creating an alternate reality, just like a dream, with your imagination.

The ideal time for reading is, unlike gaming, just before you go to sleep, because it will relax you. As with gaming, the best books to induce great dreams are ones that incite an emotional response. However, any novel offering you an escape into a reality different from your everyday life works a treat.

Your choice will be deeply personal, but to get you thinking along the right lines, here are some famous novels with plots that were actually inspired by a vision the author had in a dream. Imagine if you developed the themes of your dreams into products. Perhaps they could also become a great novel, or a TV series, a painting, an invention, a song, a film, fragrance[6] or video game! Some examples are: Dali's painting *The Persistence of Memory*; Paul McCartney's song 'Yesterday', which he heard in a dream; and the fighting robot dreamed by James Cameron that became the film *The Terminator*. Larry Page's invention of Google was triggered by a dream, and both the Theory of Relativity and the discovery of the atom's structure were inspired by dreams. It seems that in the suspended-logic world of the dream, creative connections that waking reason and disbelief typically suppress just happen. Let this list of books inspired by dreams encourage you never to dismiss your dreams as meaningless again:

Beyond the Wall of Sleep by H. P. Lovecraft
A Christmas Carol by Charles Dickens
Frankenstein by Mary Shelley
The Metamorphosis by Franz Kafka
Misery and *Dreamcatcher* by Stephen King
The Returned by Jason Mott
Sophie's Choice by William Styron
The Strange Case of Dr Jekyll and Mr Hyde by Robert Louis Stevenson
Behind Her Eyes by Sarah Pinborough
Zone One by Colson Whitehead

There's a universe of great fiction you can escape into out there, whether dreams are a theme in them or not. Keep reading to find the books of your dreams.

MOVIE NIGHTS

As a rule of thumb, it's always best to use your brain creatively. But, like anything in life, moderation is key. Sometimes it's good to have some mental downtime, again in moderation – say, one or two hours a day. Your brain does need to take a break on a daily basis to generate new ideas. You may think you are switching off or being lazy when you do something mindless like watching TV, but your brain never really switches off completely. In fact, it is recharging while you're 'doing nothing', so a little bit of laziness can be a good thing. And what better way to recharge your mind than to watch or rewatch a great movie, because a sign of a great film is that each time you watch it you discover something new.

Anything that sweeps you away to another reality and is rich in symbolism is a great treat for your 'night vision'. TV series with fantasy, supernormal or video-game inspired themes, such as *Game of Thrones* or *The Witcher* may also do the trick. Best not to watch anything an hour or so before you go to bed, though, as screens and the adrenaline rush of some shows can keep you wide awake when you need to be busy dreaming.

Here are some of my all-time favourite movies – many with

obvious dream and lucid dream themes – that often reappear in my own night visions:

> *Avatar* (2009) / *Inception* (2010) / *Inside Out* (2015) / *The Lord of the Rings* trilogy (2001–3) / The Marvel Cinematic Universe series (2008 to present) / *The Matrix* trilogy (1999–2003) / *Pan's Labyrinth* (2006) / *Soul* (2020) / *Vanilla Sky* (2001) / *What Dreams May Come* (1998)

BIGGER DREAM TIPS

- Remember, you're never too old to learn something new. If you don't believe me, google the YouTube gamer Shirley Curry, known as 'Skyrim Granny'.
- Don't think you have enough time to game, watch TV or read a book? Try to stop passively scrolling on the newsfeed!
- Prone to nightmares? You can choose family-friendly games, books and TV programmes that tone down gore, violence and sex. It's a matter of personal taste, but whatever you decide, know that facing your deepest fears, whether in games, dreams or your waking life, is a way to disarm them.
- Playing games from the first-person perspective is ideal, but playing any kind of immersive video game mimics your dreaming life.
- The more emotional or fear-inducing the game is, the better.

- Single-player games tend to be best for aiding lucid dreaming, as, like dreams, these experiences are personal to you and have no outside interference.
- Around thirty minutes of gaming each day is ideal, and you should play for no longer than an hour. As you fall deep into another reality, sense how powerful this exercise is for boosting your creativity, sense of possibility and night visions.
- Once your total immersion time is up, *stop*. It's time to immerse yourself in your waking life again.
- If you know you have an addictive personality, put a one-hour limit on your gaming time. Before you start, set a timer, and when the timer goes off, stop gaming and return to your daily routine. Should you find yourself wanting to play for much longer than that, choose one of the non-video gaming options.

Your Dream Works: *Total Immersion*

WHAT YOU'VE LEARNED: Your brain needs creative stimulation and 'practise' in an alternate reality when you are awake to encourage it to send you fantastical dreams.

TAKE NOTE: Keep a list of games, stories or TV series that have inspired you, particularly if they have triggered a vivid dream. Use this to curate your total immersion experience.

#2

Brain Charge

The more you challenge your brain and unlock its unlimited potential during the day, the more 'awake' your mind is likely to be at night. Approaching things in a new way keeps your brain on high alert.[7] The busier your brain is, the more rewarding your life. And the more rewarding your life, the more fulfilling your dreaming, as your dreams reflect who you are during the day.

In essence, the more routine, predictable and in a rut your waking life is, the less likely you are to have memorable dreams. If you want your dreaming – and your life – to upgrade, it's high time to shake up and recharge your brain.

FIND YOUR WAY

OUT OF TIME

Here's an exercise that can help you cultivate an optimum dream-inducing mindset. Asking your brain to remember your waking reality in backwards order challenges the supremacy of the logical or rational side of your brain, the left brain, which feels comfortable with order.

When you are awake, your logical left brain tends to dominate or overshadow the more imaginative, creative and intuitive right brain, which is where all inspiration comes from. But when you're asleep, your intuition is freed from restraints and speaks to you in the symbolic language of dreams.

That's why, as you may have noticed, your dreams don't obey the linear, logical or rational laws that govern your waking reality. They spring from an alternate reality where there is no order or sense of time or space, or any rules or rationality at all. While you are sleeping, your imagination is unchained.

Performing this backward-thinking exercise completely blind-sides your logical brain. It sends a strong message to your intuitive right brain that you are willing to override logic and are therefore receptive to any messages it feels inspired to send you in your dreams.

How do you do it? Half an hour or so before you go to bed, you try to remember your day in reverse order.

- Set a timer on your phone or watch for one minute.

- Take a deep breath, close your eyes and focus your concentration.

- Tell yourself that on the count of three you are going to remember what happened in your day in reverse order.

- Start from the half an hour or so before you get ready for bed and go back to when you got up in the morning.
- See yourself getting ready to go to bed, then reflect on your evening meal. Don't focus on daily trivia, just the focal points of your day – the key moments.
- Next, backtrack to how you spent your afternoon.
- Then what you ate for lunch.
- Keep going back over your morning and waking-up routine.
- End this exercise with remembering any dreams you recalled first thing in the morning.
- Stop when your timer goes off.

This sounds simple. In fact, it is anything but. If you've ever tried writing with your non-dominant hand, you'll be familiar with the sense of awkwardness and unfamiliarity you will experience.

It's also virtually impossible to do this exercise flawlessly first time around. You'll notice that your mind immediately wants to impose a logical order and think forwards, not backwards. If this happens, don't get tense. The aim is to achieve sixty seconds of fluent backwards thinking. But even if you only achieve ten-second bursts, that's enough to send your brain a powerful message that you are serious about empowering your intuitive, dreaming mind so that it isn't constantly overshadowed by logic and linear time.

If you keep repeating the exercise every evening, ideally for twenty-one days, you'll find that you gradually adjust and it feels easier and more natural. When that happens, give yourself a huge pat on the back. You are really shaking up your mind and can expect to see positive changes in both your waking life and your dreams.

BIGGER DREAM TIP

- If performing *Out of Time* before you go to sleep wakes you up, do it in the morning instead. You can also use it whenever you need to brainstorm or you feel mentally stuck. It's very refreshing and boosts creativity – like taking a mental cold shower.

BRAIN TEASERS

Don't just stop with thinking backwards. There are plenty of other effective ways to view your life in a non-linear or logical way. Brain training is big business these days and there are lots of apps and books of exercises available. Experiment to find what works for you, but do make sure that the training doesn't just focus on boosting your left-brain logic, memory and concentration. It should also include exercises that will enhance your right-brain creativity and intuition. Some examples that will help you take a fresh perspective on life:

- Have you ever tried to read upside down? Try with this book now. Turn it upside down. Start with a few sentences and gradually move on to reading a whole paragraph.
- Trying writing with your non-dominant hand.
- Take a different route to work.
- Sit at a different place at your dining table.
- Learn a new language.

THINK UP, THINK DOWN

Poetry tends to defy logic, time and space and presents symbols, metaphors, images and fragments, rather like a dream. Reading and/or writing poetry can encourage suspension of disbelief.

The glorious Dr Seuss quote on thinking left and thinking right, or down when you want to think up, is pure dream speak.

Coleridge's *Kubla Khan* is a sublime poem that was inspired by a vision in a dream. Seek it out. Read it out loud. Savour every evocative dream-inducing word.

The Life Review

Interestingly, accounts of near-death experiences (NDEs) often feature a life review, where in the 'afterlife' a person sees their life in reverse. In an NDE a person technically dies, in that their heart, lungs and brain shut down, but when resuscitated, they share memories of travelling out of their body into another reality that defies the laws of time and space. There's a growing amount of anecdotal evidence for NDEs and some credible scientific research. The reality these people say they experience is most definitely non-linear.

Some cultures and mystics believe that dreams are the door to the afterlife, and every night when you go to sleep, you 'die' and visit the other side. Every morning when you wake up, you are born anew. What a beautiful, mind-blowing thought!

Your Dream Works: *Brain Charge*

WHAT YOU'VE LEARNED: You can challenge the dominance of your brain's preferred logical and linear way of thinking when you are awake as well as in your dreams.

TAKE NOTE: See if there is any correlation between the brain-training exercises you are doing and any shimmering new perspectives emerging in your thinking. Immediately write down any insights that come to you. Otherwise, like fleeting dreams, they might slip away.

3

Imaginators

When you dream, your imagination has free rein. It is no longer restrained by the logic that dominates your waking hours. If 'imagination' is a word that feels vague, unreal and not that important to you when your eyes are open, chances are you'll have a similarly dismissive attitude towards your dreams. Your logical and rational mind will just be programmed to dismiss or block whatever feels like a figment of your imagination, and that includes any dream memories that surface on waking. However, the more you use your imagination during the day, the more it will feel empowered to express itself wildly at night, when your waking mind can't contain it.

The key to empowering your imagination is to remember how to think and feel in images and symbols, as these are the language of your imagination and your dreams.

One of the most powerful ways to stimulate your imagination is visualization, which is simply picturing in your mind's eye what you want to see. Visualization is a self-help tool that is highly successful in assisting people to reach their goals.[8] It's also a great tool for feeling at ease with the creativity of your dream world.

Visualization is something children often do without consciously trying. Not surprisingly then, childhood is the time when most of us experience a rich dream life. Unless you are an artist or a highly creative individual, though, chances are you've seriously neglected the power of visualization over the years since then. At school you were probably not encouraged to value your imagination. Tangible, hard facts and logic were considered of more value in life than the unseen and 'irrational'. But as imagination and vivid dreams go hand in hand, it's high time to think about balancing the scales. Not to mention that there's a proven link[9] between dream recall and greater creativity.

FIND YOUR WAY

PICTURE IMPERFECT

Many an artist has visualized their work before creating it and many an entrepreneur or inventor has initiated a business or made great progress through seeing a picture of what they wanted to achieve in their mind. But imagination isn't reserved for the 'gifted, creative elite'. Neither is it a refuge for drifters who want to escape from the hard facts of daily life. It is the driving force behind dreams.

Picture Imperfect is a powerful daily visualization exercise you can do to remind your waking, rational brain that your imagination is a potent creative force to be respected and reckoned with. The better your visualization skills in waking life, the clearer your mind pictures will become when you're dreaming. As visualization can sound rather esoteric or intangible, and you may need a little help getting used to it, this exercise will offer you an external catalyst. You'll need about five minutes to perform it. It's one you are encouraged to practise daily so that it becomes easier and easier.

- Simply search online for a painting by Monet or Renoir.
- Once you have found an image that speaks to you, set a timer for two minutes and study the image.
- Close your eyes and visualize that picture, seeing it again in your mind's eye.
- Once you start to see the image forming, try to hold on to it as long as you can.
- Notice the feelings and associations it inspires in you.
- Add in your own colour and ideas, bring it to life in your own way.
- When it fades, open your eyes and look again at the physical image.
- Did your visualization capture the painting's essence? Did your mind meld with the picture?

At first you may only be able to hold the image in your mind's eye for a few moments, but practice can make perfect.

- Once you feel confident you can capture and hold a memorable image in your mind's eye, visualize it growing larger and larger before you, until it is the size of a big screen.
- Then walk into the image and start interacting with it. What can you see or find there? Is there someone you can talk to? There's no limit to what you can add or do inside that painting.
- When you are ready to re-emerge, simply shrink the image back to its normal size and open your eyes.

This visualization is ideal before you go to sleep. But the beauty of it is that it can be performed at any time of the day, anywhere. All you need is a moment of peace and silence to explore a picture with your mind and treasure it as the stuff of many wonderful dreams to come.

MEMORY LANES

Visualization comes easier to some people than others, and there is a rare condition called aphantasia, which is the inability to visualize.[10] The good news is that aphantasia doesn't seem to impair creativity or the ability to recall dreams, and if you do have it, there are other ways to imagine that you may not have thought of as visualization before. Instead of trying to conjure images or pictures in your mind, describe them verbally instead.

- Write down or record in a voice note everything you can remember about a picture or image.

- Pretend to be an art critic describing the image for a potential buyer or reviewing it for an art magazine.

- Then, when you have remembered and described verbally all you can about the picture, add in figments of your own creativity and bring the picture to life in your own words.

BIGGER DREAM TIPS

- When you visualize, try to view a scene from your own perspective rather than if you are watching it in a movie.
- Use all your senses, not just the visual. What are you hearing, touching, tasting, smelling?
- Imagination and the ability to visualize can be casualties of busy modern life. If you find visualization frustrating, don't give up. Aim to do it in ten- or twenty-second bursts until it becomes easier.

PAINT YOUR PICTURE

Alternatively, you may want to have a go at drawing or painting the picture you want to conjure up. Don't worry about creating a work of art, just let your memories and then your imagination flow free. No one ever needs to see this picture but you and your dreaming mind!

Night and Day Visions

There's a reason I asked you to choose a Monet or a Renoir – they are famous Impressionist painters. Impressionism is a style that originated in France in the 1860s and seeks to capture the feeling or essence of a scene or person rather than a lifelike depiction. That's right. It's a dream-like style of painting. But don't feel you need to stick with the Impressionist artists. Art ignites the imagination and evokes emotion without the use of words in much the same way that a dream does, so any artwork that captures your imagination can be used for this exercise. The archetypal symbols of the Tarot cards can work wonders, as can illustrations in books of fairy tales.

You'll find that the more you practise – the more you start capturing images in your mind's eye and noticing the feelings and associations those images ignite in you – the more you will go about your daily life with the vision of an artist and 'see' this vision reflected in your dreams.

Interestingly, many of the Surrealist paintings of Salvador Dali were inspired by his dreams, to the extent that he once described his art as 'hand-painted dream photographs'. It's well worth adding visual memories of some of Dali's paintings to your dream memory collection, too.

Your Dream Works: *Imaginators*

WHAT YOU'VE LEARNED: The easier it is for you to visualize when you're awake, the more you're strengthening your imagination and giving your dreaming mind licence to thrill.

TAKE NOTE: Write down the feelings that visualizing a specific painting evokes in you. These emotions will inform your dreams. Particularly note any feelings of awe, as awe connects you to something bigger than yourself.

4

REM Expansion

If someone kept ignoring you or, when you did speak, belittled you, wouldn't you eventually want to avoid that person? Think of your dreaming mind in the same way. If you have repeatedly dismissed your dreams as nonsense, or haven't even been recalling them, you urgently need to reassure your dreaming mind that you are receptive to its precious wisdom. The previous three suggestions were all designed to give your dreaming mind an attention boost. Now that you're working every day on reassuring your dreaming mind of its importance to you, it's high time to introduce a dose of practicality.

Contrary to what you may believe, a rich dream life isn't about disconnecting from reality or reason. It is about balancing logic with creativity, seeing your waking life as an opportunity to feed your dreams and those dreams as an opportunity to inspire your life. As you'll learn in the next couple of weeks, learning how to recognize you are dreaming while you are dreaming requires a very logical mindset. So, whereas the previous exercises were about dream 'practice' and nurturing your waking creativity, *REM Expansion* is going to speak directly to your common sense.

If you routinely wake up feeling groggy, with poor dream recall, it's obvious you haven't had a good night's sleep. And if you aren't sleeping well, you aren't getting enough REM sleep – 'rapid eye movement' sleep, when your heart rate increases and your eyes dart behind closed eyelids.[11] Dreams happen in all stages of sleep, but most frequently during REM. This is the last stage of the sleep cycle and it occurs more often during the second half of the night. That's why you tend to recall dreams better when you wake up early in the morning. Ideally, you should be getting around 100 minutes of REM sleep every night.

Sleep isn't just about dreaming, though. It's healthy and healing for your mind, body and soul. You need quality, non-REM sleep to stimulate cell repair and regulate your bodily functions. Every stage of sleep matters. But the REM stage plays a crucial role in memory and healthy cognitive function, as well as mood regulation. As well as being when you dream the most, it's the stage during which, if you awaken, you are most likely to recall your dreams.

So, if you want to increase your chances of dream recall, a common-sense approach is to do all you can to extend the amount of time you spend in REM sleep.

FIND YOUR WAY

JUST MAKE YOUR BED

One of the most obvious reasons you may not be getting enough REM sleep is that the bed you are sleeping in isn't welcoming or comfortable. There are many other things that could be triggering a bad night's sleep with the resulting low REM, and they're covered below. But making your bed beautifully every day is something simple and immediate you can do to dramatically improve your sleep and time spent in REM.

There's more to this than you might think. There's a reason why there is such emphasis on making your bed in the military.[12] It is a sign of discipline that sets the right tone for the rest of the day. It also turns your attention to your bedroom and how calm and comforting it is. Last, but by no means least, it is a sign of self-care. There's nothing more stress-inducing than having to make your bed at the end of the day. By contrast, few things in life match the pleasure of climbing into a beautifully made bed at the end of a busy day.

It's easy not to bother to make your bed and to come up with all sorts of excuses, but it's equally easy to do it and to start your day – and the rest of your life – the right way. Making your bed daily is perhaps the simplest thing you can do to boost your chances of success during the day and dreams at night. It's also a daily reminder of the importance of getting a good night's sleep and will motivate you to take other positive steps to improve your sleep 'hygiene' – the behaviour and environment that you cultivate to encourage healthy rest.

So, turn this routine chore into a mindful ritual and make your bed with loving care and attention to detail:

- As you plump your pillows and smooth your sheets and duvet, focus your thoughts on why accomplishing this task matters so much.

- Remind yourself that you are setting a calm, disciplined tone for the rest of the day and are also increasing your chances of getting a good night's sleep and having wonderful dreams.

- If your bedding isn't clean or fresh smelling, make sure you change it. The same goes for your bedclothes.

- Comfort and pleasure are key. Silk pillowcases are a mini-indulgence I highly recommend. You'll reap the benefits in your skin and your dreams.

- Do all you can to make sure that your bed is as delicious and welcoming a place as possible for you to sleep and dream in.

SWEETER SLEEP STEPS

Love your bed but still can't sleep? A well-made, comfy bed may be all you need to drift off into blissful sleep, but if you still can't sleep, you might want to take a careful look at your routine. Your brain can't just jump right into sleep mode without a wind-down period. So, examine what you are doing in the hour before bed. You should avoid stimulating activities such as answering emails, watching TV, scrolling online or using electronics of any kind at least thirty minutes before lights out. Try listening to relaxing music or a podcast instead.

Journaling and meditation before bedtime are other proven ways to de-stress before sleep. Aromatherapy and sleep mists can work a treat, too. I always put a few sprinkles of lavender essential oil on my pillow. You might also like to try rose, sandalwood, mugwort, valerian, anise, clove, clary sage, bergamot or chamomile, all of which may have superior sleep-inducing properties.

Dimming the lights also helps signal to your body that it is time to wind down. Be aware that your bedroom needs to be dark enough to encourage sleep, so make sure your curtains block out the light. If that isn't possible, you might want to invest in a soft eye mask. If noise is a problem, consider ear plugs.

The optimum temperature for sleeping is cooler than you might think – around 18°C (65°F). Your body temperature drops at night and a lower temperature signals to your brain that it is time to slumber.

Everyone's sleep needs are different, but aim to go to bed at the same time each night – preferably before midnight – and to get up seven or eight hours later. If you keep doing this, your body will adjust and settle, and you will effortlessly enter the light, deep and REM stages of sleep. Waking up without an alarm will be easier too, which, as you'll see later (*page 47*), is beneficial for dream recall.

Your brain loves variety, but your body needs routine, and this is especially the case when it comes to getting quality sleep. Any change in your sleeping and waking routine will disrupt your body's rhythms and make it harder for you to get a restful night's sleep with sweet dreams. In a way, you'll suffer from jet-lag without the holiday. If you live in a country where the clock changes twice a year, it can take a while to adjust. Also, if you 'treat' yourself to a lie-in over the weekend, it might just have the opposite effect and cause fatigue. If you feel you need to catch up on sleep, by far the best option is to go to bed earlier.

There is some research[13] to suggest that around a ten-minute snooze in the morning after first waking and before you get up can trigger vivid dreaming, as your brain is conscious enough to remember your REM dreams. But lie-ins and snoozing have a way of disrupting your sleep schedule, so I suggest avoiding them the majority of the time.

You spend around a third of your life sleeping, so why not start thinking of sleep not as a waste of time but as a precious use of it. Sleeping is nightly therapy for your mind, body and soul, so treat it as sacred.

LIGHTEN UP

Getting natural daylight in the morning encourages the release of hormones that trigger a good night's sleep. So, open the curtains, or better still, step outside and let the daylight in. Fresh air, too, is a good health and better sleep tonic.

Along with daylight, gentle exercise – just brisk walking for twenty minutes a day or doing any light physical movement, such as yoga, jogging, dancing or swimming – is beneficial for *REM Expansion*. A gym is great, but outdoor exercise adds the dream-boosting benefits of daylight. Do make sure, though, that you take your exercise at least two hours before bedtime, otherwise the activity could wake you up too much.

BIGGER DREAM TIPS

- If your mind is still active or you wake up feeling restless with your mind racing in the night, don't lie awake in bed, because that will lead your brain to believe that your bed isn't a place for sleeping. The best thing to do is to get up and read or journal.
- Scared of nightmares? Cutting down on stress and having a bedtime routine can diminish the risk of nightmares. But if they do strike, I hope working through this book will change your perspective on dreaming, so you regard every dream,

including your nightmares (*see page 160*), as a healing gift for you to decode.

- If you work a night shift or your partner is a restless sleeper and wakes you up, sleep hygiene can be more challenging. But you can still make your bed on waking and initiate a bedtime routine if you work night shifts. And if your partner is making it impossible for you to sleep, you could consider sleeping separately for the sake of your health (and your relationship).
- Bear in mind, too, that if you are on medication, suffer from sleep apnoea (a condition where you briefly pause your breathing intermittently while asleep) or have health problems, these can also minimize time spent dreaming.

Track your REM Sleep

A sure-fire indicator of getting enough REM sleep is clear dream recall. You can also find out if you are managing this by using one of the free apps that monitor your sleep. SleepScore is the one I use. These apps will tell you how many minutes you spent in the REM stage, and they may also offer comparisons with others your age and gender, as well as giving you lots of other healthy sleeping tips. It can get quite addictive finding out what you got up to at night, but anything that encourages you to enjoy sleeping more is a bonus. Apple Watch and Fitbits can also track your sleep stages, including REM. While you sleep, these devices monitor how your heart rate changes when you move between sleep stages.

Your Dream Works: *REM Expansion*

WHAT YOU'VE LEARNED: Making your bed every day and paying closer attention to your sleep hygiene not only improves the quality of your sleep and your well-being during the day, but also dramatically increases your chances of getting enough REM time to dream in.

TAKE NOTE: Write down the impact your sleep hygiene has on your sleep and your life. Do you feel brighter in the day? Are clearer fragments of dreams shining through?

5

Eat your Dreams

You may be surprised to learn that your diet can have a significant effect on dreaming. Certain nutrients may boost your dream recall and also help to transform regular dreaming into lucid dreaming. *Eat your Dreams* will draw your attention to these dream-inducing nutrients and also explain what the optimum diet for your dreams should be.

Eating cheese just before you go to sleep is commonly believed to give you nightmares. This is actually a myth, but, like many myths, it's based on truth. It's not the cheese that's triggering nightmares but a full stomach, as cheese takes a while to digest. If you go to bed while your stomach is digesting heavy or spicy food or alcohol, your sleep is going to be lighter and you are more likely to spend time in REM sleep and so have vivid dreams. Whether those dreams transform into nightmares or not depends on your underlying anxiety levels at the time, not the cheese!

It's easy, therefore, to think then that going to bed with a full stomach is a good thing, as it extends your REM time. However, you'd be making a big mistake. The best recipe for wonderful dreaming is a good night's sleep. If your sleep is light and restless, because you're busy digesting food, you won't be reaching the deep stages of sleep you need in order to wake up feeling refreshed. And if you do recall more of your dreams on waking, you won't be in the relaxed frame of mind to understand them and get the best out of them. It's *quality, not quantity*, that counts when it comes to your dreams. You want dreams that can inform, inspire and energize your waking life – dreams so magical that you wake up bursting with creativity and motivation. As the last practice explained (*see page 33*), you won't have those life-enhancing dreams if your sleep hygiene is poor.

It is often said you are what you eat. I believe you are what you dream. There is a strong connection between healthy eating and sweet dreams, so eating well is a firm foundation for great dreams. You need to make sure that your diet doesn't lack the nutrients that have been clearly associated with better dream recall. These nutrients are your dream food.

FIND YOUR WAY

GET YOUR VITAMIN B

Vitamin B6 is strongly associated with dream recall because it is needed for proper brain and memory function, mood regulation and energy metabolism. It also helps make the hormones that regulate your internal clock and your sleep, which also maintain healthy skin, hair and vision.

Research has shown that if people are given vitamin B6 supplements before they go to sleep, they remember more dreams and have an increased incidence of lucid dreams. In one study, participants who took vitamin B6 for four nights in a row before going to bed had significantly clearer dream recall on waking.[14]

Given this research, B6 supplements are an option you might want to consider in the short term to give your dream recall a jump start. But only in the short term, because nutritionists agree that by far the best way to get essential nutrients is through the food you eat every day, not through taking a pill.

In addition, the eight B vitamins work synergistically, so taking a B6 supplement isn't going to be that effective if you are lacking other B vitamins in your diet.

If you do decide to supplement with vitamin B, be sure to check with your doctor that it is safe for you to do so, especially if you are pregnant or on medication. And don't take over 100mg of vitamin B6 a day.

B-rich Foods

The B vitamins are water soluble, meaning they dissolve in water, so any excess gets excreted in urine. That means you need to eat foods rich in vitamin B every single day, because your body can't store it. To ensure you are getting your Bs, your diet should include the following excellent sources of these vitamins:

dark green leafy vegetables such as spinach and broccoli
fruit such as bananas and avocados
seeds and nuts such as sunflower seeds and almonds
legumes such as beans and lentils
pork, chicken, eggs, milk or non-meat and dairy alternatives such as soya beans if you are vegetarian or vegan
oats and fortified breakfast cereals

If you are a vegetarian or vegan or don't eat much protein, you need to pay special attention to how much vitamin B you are getting every day, because meat, poultry and fish are rich sources of B6. Make extra sure you eat plenty of wholegrains, fortified cereals, nuts, beans, bananas and potatoes.

Whenever you are eating a source of vitamin B, take your time to chew it mindfully. Put your knife and fork down between bites, and as you eat it, remind yourself that you are feeding your brain dream food.

Mind your Bs

If you suffer from anaemia, mouth ulcers, soreness and cracks around the corners of your mouth, chapped lips, tingling or numbness in your hands or feet, confusion, irritability, depression, forgetfulness, unsteadiness or poor coordination, it's possible this could be linked to vitamin B deficiency. If you decide to take a supplement, the optimum time is after your evening meal on a full stomach. Vitamin B6 is typically included in a good multivitamin, or you can purchase individual B-complex vitamins or B6 supplements. Check with your doctor before taking a supplement. And remember, around 100mg a day of B6 is advised for adults and no more than that. Taking too many B6 supplements for a year or so can lead to nerve damage, so be absolutely sure not to overdo it.

A BALANCED DIET

To ensure your diet is dream friendly, you first need to make sure it is healthy and balanced. This means eating as wide a variety of foods as possible from all the important food groups and eating them in the right proportions to maintain a healthy weight. There is plenty of professional advice out there on healthy eating, so seek it out. There's also lots of advice on the best nutrients to ensure a good night's sleep. Calcium (found in milk and almonds) and magnesium (dark green leafy veg) are associated with restful sleep.

Foods containing melatonin, a hormone that improves sleep quality, may also help. Melatonin is found in eggs, fish, milk and nuts. A light snack of foods known to encourage relaxation, such as almonds, walnuts or oatmeal biscuits with a little marmite or clear natural honey just before you go to bed can also be helpful. Or you could simply have a glass of warm milk or a cup of relaxing herbal tea – for example, chamomile, valerian root, lavender or lemon balm.

BIGGER DREAM TIPS

- Leave yourself a good two hours to digest your food properly before you go to sleep.
- If you regularly get in late and eating your main meal late at night is the only option, at least try to ensure that your supper isn't heavy.
- During the day, try to eat a healthy lunch and don't be tempted to skip breakfast. It really is the most important meal of the day. As the saying goes, it's best to breakfast like a king (or queen), lunch like a prince (or princess) and dine like a pauper.
- Also avoid alcohol and caffeine before bedtime, as they are both toxins your body and brain don't want or need.

Blue Pill, Red Pill?

Perhaps you've come across herbs and supplements on the market today that claim to increase dream recall and lucidity. Many herbs, such as *Silene capensis* (African dream root, which is, unusually, taken in the morning rather than at night), *Calea zacatechichi* (Mexican dream plant), blue lotus, camalonga and mugwort, are used in the spiritual rituals of indigenous dreaming cultures. They can all help boost the levels of neurotransmitters in your brain.

Melatonin supplements, which are often prescribed for insomnia, have also been associated with more vivid dreaming, as have B vitamin supplements (*see above*) and Huperxine A, the sesquiterpene alkaloid compound that is extracted from Chinese club moss (*Huperzia serrata*) and believed to boost memories.

Some companies claim to have created a special supplement with natural chemical additions to boost lucid dreaming, although the evidence is largely anecdotal. Be aware, too, that dream-inducing supplements seriously disrupt sleep, because they require you to sleep for a few hours, then wake up and take them before going back to sleep. This 'wake up, go back to bed' technique is likely to increase the amount of REM sleep you have anyway, so there's a placebo effect here.

You might be tempted to take lucid dreaming supplements to get a more intense dream experience. They offer you an immediate glimpse of lucidity to inspire you. But my strong advice is to avoid any quick fix or any kind of dependency on herbs or supplements that claim to help you dream better, certainly in the long term. If you do want to experiment with a supplement, think of it as a one-off and always, always consult your doctor first, as there could be contraindications or unpleasant side-effects. You have within you all that you need to dream bigger and better. Your dreaming mind knows that. You need to comprehend that too.

Your Dream Works: *Eat your Dreams*

WHAT YOU'VE LEARNED: Make sure your diet is healthy and you get enough vitamin B in your diet every day. This will ensure healthy brain and body function. Keep an eye on what foods best feed your dreams.

TAKE NOTE: Keep a food diary and write down how many foods rich in vitamin B6 you eat each day. Notice how what you eat during the day impacts your dreams at night. See, over time, if you can identify which B-vitamin food sources are most associated with clear dream recall on awakening and perhaps also help you turn regular dreams into lucid ones.

6

First Things First

Immediately on waking you are in that twilight stage between sleep and wakefulness. Sometimes it can be hard to know the difference between your dreams and reality in this stage. The reason for this is that your brainwaves are in theta mode. Delta is the stage when you are fast asleep. Theta is when you are relaxed just before sleeping or just after waking. (Alpha is when you are calm and awake; beta is when you are fully awake and active, with gamma being a state of intense concentration and alertness.)

Theta brainwaves are the optimum state for recalling dreams and reprogramming your mind. When you are fully awake and your brain becomes more alert in alpha, beta and gamma, your brain is just not as receptive to dream recall. So, what you think about on waking can be potentially life-changing. It's also why this time – when you are as close as possible to your dreams – is the perfect time to gently reach for them.

Although a dream can pop into your mind later in the day when something you see, think about or sense triggers a dream memory, dream recall tends to occur within the first thirty minutes after waking, with the first two minutes being the most likely time.

What you may not realize is that everything you are currently doing in those first thirty minutes on waking might be the enemy of dream recall. But there is something you can do to significantly increase your chances of better dream recall. *You just need to keep calm and still.*

FIND YOUR WAY

DON'T BLINK

If you are practising the sleep hygiene tips given in *REM Expansion* (*see page* 33), you will ideally be waking up around the same time each day without an alarm. That's the optimum way to wake up for dream recall, because an alarm of any kind thrusts you rudely into the land of waking and doesn't give you any transition time to gently recall your dreams.

Your dreaming mind struggles to make its presence felt when your conscious mind takes over, with all the logic and endless 'to dos' that come with waking awareness. Also, movement increases your level of alertness and moves you right out of theta. It also signals to your brain that it is time to rise and get busy. So, what you need to do is stay a little longer in the shadows with your dreams.

Keeping your eyes closed fools your brain into thinking you are still asleep and dreaming. Opening your eyes and blinking will decrease your chances of dream recall. A fascinating study has shown that every time you blink, your brain redirects its attention.[15] You want to focus your brain's attention on your dreams as long as possible, so try to avoid blinking and follow this sequence on waking:

- Keep your eyes closed and aim to stay exactly in the position you woke up in for around ninety seconds.
- As you lie there, just let your thoughts take you back to the land of your dreams.
- Ask for dream memories, or focus on one question (only): *What can I remember from my dreams?*
- Notice whatever images, symbols or sensations come up. See them on the backs of your eyelids if you can.
- If nothing comes through, check in with your feelings, as these will also be symptoms of a dream.
- Do a body scan to see if there is any tension in your body, as your intuition will often speak to you that way.
- Then, when images come flooding in, just let them come alive. Don't try to analyse or interpret or make sense of them at this stage; simply relish and relive the memories.

TAKE THIRTY

It's easy to forget to keep still in the first few minutes of waking, but don't despair if this doesn't work for you. Dream recall is also likely in the first thirty minutes after you awake, so optimize that time too. Whatever your morning routine, try to ensure that in those first thirty minutes you don't reach for your phone. As soon as you do that, you shift your focus from your own needs to the needs of others or to your newsfeed. Checking your phone will put a damper on the mood of your whole day. It will also drive any dream recall away.

Instead of worrying about your phone, do a glorious whole-body stretch and yawn when you first get out of bed. Not only is this energizing, but it may also encourage more expansive thinking. And wherever your thinking is expansive, your dreams aren't far behind. Yes, your mind influences your body, but your body also influences your mind. It's amazing how many of us minimize ourselves physically when we get out of bed in the morning, and our mind will follow suit.

So, in those precious early morning moments that set the tone for your day, focus on *your* needs, on who you are, on your dreams. It really is crucial, both for your dream recall and for your life in general, that you put yourself centre stage in what many highly successful people call their 'power hour'. Acknowledging your own needs first and foremost isn't selfish. In fact, it's the most unselfish thing you can do, because you can't give to others what you don't have yourself.

BIGGER DREAM TIPS

- You might wake up bursting to go to the bathroom. If nature is calling you, of course you need to answer it. You can return to bed after you have used the bathroom and close your eyes to see if any dreams and reflections come to you.
- Try not to sleep with your phone (or any other electrics) charging right beside you. Ideally, keep them in another room.

Eureka!

You may well find as you go about your usual morning routine, in particular when you shower, that dream memories suddenly break through like a rainbow after rain. Your conscious awareness is on autopilot when you perform activities such as showering, walking, driving or sitting on a train, and this offers your dreams a chance to take centre stage.

If dream memories bubble through in your morning routine, or anytime later in the day, write them down instantly or they will fly away. Don't worry at this stage about understanding or decoding them. Don't try to make any sense of them either. They won't make sense just yet. At the start of week three you'll acquire some fantastic tools to help you become your own dream oracle. Right now, your focus should just be on catching those dreams and savouring them.

Your Dream Works: *First Things First*

WHAT YOU'VE LEARNED: The thread connecting you to your dreams is strongest when you wake. So stay still and recall what you can. Any activity that focuses on the busy day ahead will push your dreams into the background, where they are easily forgotten.

TAKE NOTE: Notice how staying calm first thing contributes to better dream recall and/or early morning inspirations. Write down whatever you recall or feel. You could even practise Julia Cameron's Morning Pages, writing three A4 pages of whatever comes to mind.

#7

Show (and Tell) Yourself

I hope by now you have realized that you can change your dreams and your life for the better by changing your waking perspective and routine. I also hope that you grasp that the only person who can make that positive change is *you*. The type of person you are and the kind of dreams you have are the result of all your past experiences and perspectives, as well as all the things others have told you and you have told yourself.

Your mind can't tell the difference between fact and opinion. If you constantly tell yourself that things won't work out for you or that your dreams are meaningless, sooner or later your mind will be convinced. Don't let this make you despondent or fear your own inner voice, though. Quite the contrary. The suggestible nature of your mind is a reason to rejoice, because it means you can begin the process of positive change by altering the thoughts and words that you repeat to yourself.

One of the simplest ways to change the way your mind is programmed is through repeating positive intentions. Positive intentions interrupt negative thought patterns that have become ingrained over the years and have blunted your happiness and your dream recall. They help you replace what is not working in your best interests with something positive. They let you take control and make your thoughts work for you rather than against you. They encourage your mind to get curious, to seek out ways to fulfil your intentions and to actually create the future of your dreams.

Would you believe me if I told you that one single statement repeated nightly before you go to bed can dramatically increase your ability to recall your dreams and become lucid in them? It's true and all will be revealed below.

FIND YOUR WAY

STATE YOUR INTENTION

Thoughts without actions to back them up have no power. But upgrading your thinking just before you go to sleep is a powerful way to supercharge all the other dream recall exercises you have performed this week. This is the second magical opportunity in your day to change your life and your dreams for the better, because, as the last practice made clear, your brain is relaxing into an impressionable theta state at that time.

- Before you go to sleep each night, look at your pillow as if it were a face or a mirror and repeat in your mind the following:

'Tonight, my dreams will show themselves to me. And if the time is right for me to do so, I will become aware I am dreaming while I am dreaming. In the morning when I wake up, I will have clear dream recall.'

- Put your belief and your heart into it.

- If you feel bold enough, saying your intention out loud, rather than silently, encourages your mind to regard your statement as a fact, an absolute truth. When words don't just come from your thoughts, but also from your voice, it gives them more authority and encourages your dreaming mind to believe what you are saying. And when you speak, do so with a sense of joy and possibility. Think about the fun you can have with your dreams and the infinite surprises in store for you.

What you say out loud just before you go to bed will be stored in your unconscious, where it will inform your dreams. So, make and sleep on your intention-to-dream statement every night moving forward, so that it becomes so ingrained that your dreaming mind just accepts it.

WRITE A DREAM LETTER

If talking to yourself or your pillow, either in your thoughts or out loud, doesn't resonate with you, why not write to your dreaming mind instead?

- Simply write down your dream intention on a small piece of paper.
- Then add an extra sentence along the lines of: 'Tonight, I want to dream about...'
- In the morning, if you had a dream and you don't feel it matched your intention, look for deeper meanings in it.
- If that doesn't help, the next night ask your dreaming mind to bring you clarity. Dreams rarely occur in isolation and often comment on themselves. Think of your favourite TV series. Sometimes your dreams reveal themselves through a series of episodes in a similar fashion.
- When you have finished your letter, sign it. There is something sacred about your signature and you are now entering into a signed contract with your dreaming mind.
- You can put the note under your pillow or keep it in a drawer close to your bed.

If you still feel faintly ridiculous talking to your pillow or writing a letter to yourself, don't worry, just have a good laugh at yourself. When it comes to dream work, taking yourself a little less seriously can work wonders. As can being brave enough to experiment with new techniques. You have nothing to lose and everything to gain by giving it a try!

Intentions

There's real science and psychology behind the power of intention. Research has shown that, like prayer, repeating intentions using positive affirmations can help rewire your brain.[16] Of course, powerful thoughts without positive actions to validate and complete them won't work. But upgrading your thinking about your dream recall can really supercharge your efforts. Affirmations work by interrupting and overriding negative beliefs or thoughts that are creating mental blocks and replacing them with positive ones – in this case, dream-inducing ones. In short, they make your waking and dreaming mind work for you rather than against you.

Your Dream Works: *Show (and Tell) Yourself*

WHAT YOU'VE LEARNED: Your mind believes what you tell it repeatedly and is highly suggestible before sleep. Keep saying you are going to remember your dreams before you go to sleep and sooner or later you will.

TAKE NOTE: Use the power of intention every night before you go to sleep to make your agreement with your dreaming mind formal and official. From now on, believe absolutely and completely in your ability to recall your dreams. Rest assured your dreaming mind will be taking note.

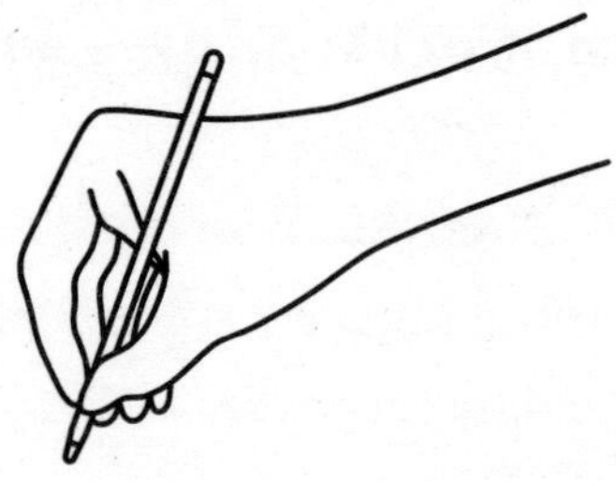

YOUR WEEK ONE DREAMER'S CHECKPOINT

This week you have been encouraged to think, feel, imagine and do things that can help you dream and live bigger and better. By now, you may be starting to recall more vivid dreams, or at the very least be waking up feeling more refreshed. If you aren't yet, don't panic. This isn't a race against anyone or anything. It's all about discovering what is best for and within *you*. Every forgotten dream, like every loss in waking life, offers you information you can learn from. So, keep practising. Keep learning what works and what doesn't. Trust that your dreams will show themselves when you are fully rested, recharged and ready. Tomorrow is another day. Perhaps your dreams will come flooding back to you then. In any event, you have the next seven days and nights of deep dreaming techniques to discover!

But before you launch into them, here's a brief overview of what you've discovered so far. You can pop a tick next to each of the techniques you've tried so you can keep track of your progress.

#1: TOTAL IMMERSION

- ○ Game Power
- ○ Lost in Words
- ○ Movie Nights

#2: BRAIN CHARGE

- ○ Out of Time
- ○ Brain Teasers
- ○ Think Up, Think Down

#3: IMAGINATORS

- ○ Picture Imperfect
- ○ Memory Lanes
- ○ Paint your Picture

#4: REM EXPANSION

- ○ Just Make your Bed
- ○ Sweeter Sleep Steps
- ○ Lighten Up

#5: EAT YOUR DREAMS

- ○ Get your Vitamin B
- ○ A Balanced Diet

#6: FIRST THINGS FIRST

- ○ Don't Blink
- ○ Take Thirty

#7: SHOW (AND TELL) YOURSELF

- ○ State your Intention
- ○ Write a Dream Letter

Dream Deeper

SEVEN WAYS TO 'LIVE' YOUR DREAMS

'Dreams feel real while we are in them. It's only when we wake up that we realize something was actually strange.'
Cobb, *Inception*

By now your dream recall may be starting to feel more consistent. You may even be beginning to relish your engrossing inner dialogue and your growing awareness of just how interconnected your waking and dreaming lives are. Any growing excitement about your dream power is a very promising sign. You are awakening to the wealth and wisdom of your own soul.

In the words of Aristotle, 'Self-knowledge is the beginning of all wisdom.' However, if you are following the Week One dream recall guidelines and your dream recall still isn't fluent, now might be the perfect time to start gently wondering why you aren't quite ready to know yourself more intimately. As always, don't judge, just start reflecting. Your earnest desire to go deeper and find answers may even prompt recall in the coming days. Any sincere and heartfelt questions you ask in your waking life, like all the other things you feel, think and do with your whole heart, are reflected back in abundant symbolic form in your dreams.

Becoming aware of your connection to your inner world and the language of your heart while awake is an absolutely crucial step that is often overlooked. Your dreaming world takes its cues from your waking life. 'Lucidity' is really just another word for awareness, or being mindful of your 'reality', and that begins not when you fall asleep but when your eyes are open. That's why the seven ways to 'live' your dreams this week focus intensely on your waking life and the things you can do to dramatically increase the likelihood of vivid dreams you don't just recall on waking, but can also, potentially, wake up in.

All these techniques are designed to be repeated daily and, as before, options are offered to help you find what works best for you. The first practice this week offers an intuitive lifestyle choice which will be a firm foundation for greater dreams. The six practices that follow add deeper and deeper layers to your days, so that your dreams can unravel at night. Above all, though, this second week of your dream adventure will fully explore the power of intuitive living to shake and wake your night vision and the power of your dreams.

In essence: great life, great dreams!

8

Spidey Sense

In your dreams, your intuition, like your creativity or imagination, has the opportunity to express itself with joyful abandon. When you're awake, your conscious mind with its rational and logical restrictions tends to overpower its subtle unconscious messages. That's why you can gather profound insights about yourself and your life in your dreams[1] that you typically can't access when you're awake.

Intuition is knowledge that isn't informed by logic, reason or even reality. It's a rapid process that occurs outside your conscious mental or logical processes. Terms such as 'gut instinct', 'sixth sense' and 'inner voice' are often used to describe it. In the military it is called 'spidey sense'. In his seminal 2005 book *Blink: The Power of Thinking Without Thinking*, Malcolm Gladwell describes intuition as something that happens behind a 'closed door', because it happens outside your conscious awareness.

You can easily mistake fear and anxiety for intuition, but there is a real difference. If fear is doing the talking, you'll feel swept away by conflicting voices and pulled down by self-judgement. You'll feel stuck, helpless, paralysed. If, on the other hand, you get a gentle and empowering feeling, your heart rate stays steady and you just know with calm certainty and conviction that you *need* to do something, don't hesitate or blink, as that's your intuition talking. Act on it. In every scientific breakthrough a leap of intuitive faith must be made for there to be progress.

We tend to think of intuition and logic as opposites, like waking life and dreams. But you shouldn't regard your intuition as separate from logic, but as an integral part of it. Intuition isn't guessing. It is often informed by and based on experiences and information stored in your long-term memory which you aren't consciously aware of and which can reveal themselves suddenly though a flash of inspiration or a vivid dream. And when you fall asleep, you don't become a different person, you just enter a different state of awareness. The more you open your mind to your intuition and trust in its power in your waking life, the more powerfully your dreams will speak to you. Intuition and dreams are just two sides of the same coin that is *you*.

Even though mundane dreams are still a priceless gift, the more you start fine-tuning and strengthening your intuition in your waking life, and the more intensely and psychologically aware you are of your surroundings, the more confidently and expressively your intuition is going to speak to you in your dreams. So, this practice encourages you to flex your intuition muscle as much as possible when you are wide awake, so that when you fall asleep your intuition is primed and ready to reveal its treasures.

FIND YOUR WAY

GET YOUR MOON FIX

If you want to boost your intuition by day, look no further than the moon.

Just as there is a clear link between the moon and dreams, because both come out at night, there's also a powerful connection in many traditions between the moon and our unconscious or inner world. Intuition is believed to spring from that world, from the shadows.

Moonology, or lunar living, is a lifestyle choice for many who believe that harnessing the power of the different phases of the moon can boost their intuition, health and happiness. If this sounds far too 'woo-woo', I urge you to take a leap of faith out of your comfort zone (remember your dreaming mind loves it when you do that) and experiment. You have nothing to lose and only illumination to gain.

In ancient times, people's lives were aligned with nature, the seasons and the moon's phases. This gave them an understanding of time and when it was optimum for them to plant, harvest, gather and perform their rituals. The gravitational pull of the moon rules the tides, stabilizes the Earth's axis and impacts the seasons, so this isn't as primitive as it may sound. And as water makes up roughly 60–70 per cent of the human body, perhaps the moon can exert a gravitational pull on us too, bringing all that is beneath our conscious awareness – our instincts, our intuitions and our dreams – to the surface.

Modern life has disrupted our ancient alignment to nature and the moon and its intuition-boosting power, but it is very easy to get back in tune with the moon. There's a wealth of information online about how best to do this – the clearer skies of the pandemic lockdowns dramatically increased people's awareness of the power of lunar living – but as with many instinctive things, it really is very simple. Here's all you need to know about lunar power and how to get your daily intuition and dream-boosting moon fix.

LUNAR CYCLES

The moon orbits the Earth. It remains whole but appears to alter its shape because each night we see different parts of the moon illuminated by sunlight. These shifting light patterns create the roughly twenty-nine-day lunar month, which is how long it takes for the moon to move around the Earth. This exercise will focus on the four major phases of the lunar month and how best to tune into them for both vivid dreams and a vibrant life. There are other intermediate and lesser-known phases that are thought to have their own vibrations, too, but awareness of the four main phases is enough for this to work.

To find out which phase of the moon you are currently in, simply do a search online. There are several websites offering information: www.timeanddate.com/moon/phases is an example. Be aware that the country you are living in needs to be taken into consideration.

Here are the phases and how best to use them:

Dark and New Moon: New Beginnings

This is when you see just a hint of the moon in the sky – a slender crescent, which is why it's sometimes called the crescent moon. The dark moon is the few days when it is barely visible at all. The absence of light can feel unsettling, but if you embrace the darkness, you can understand this is when your plans and ideas, like seeds, can be planted and given space to grow.

The new moon is the ideal time to pause and reflect, set intentions, learn new things and prepare for new beginnings. As far as your dream work is concerned, it's the ideal time to meditate, journal and prepare or set intentions to dream.

Waxing Moon: Taking Action

During this phase the moon begins to move from being hidden to being completely visible. Each night it reveals more and more reflected light, just as your dreams reveal your real life and areas that need healing. It feels reassuring to witness this visible return to strength and power. After the darkness there is new light and hope, and this can inspire you to move your plans from the unseen world of possibility to the visible world of action. Determined focus and practical and positive action should move centre stage now, in your life as well as in all your dream work.

Full Moon: Dreaming Heights

This is the most powerful phase of the lunar cycle, when lunar energy is at its peak. It typically happens around fifteen to eighteen days after a new moon and is the time when you can see the whole moon in the sky.

The full moon is a time of creativity and celebration, but do watch out for sensitivity and stress. Many people report feeling emotional at this time, which is why the full moon is often associated with 'lunacy' (from 'lunar'). They also report having far more frequent and intense dreams. Channel this emotional intensity into your dream work, so it can help you embrace what heals rather than harms you.

Waning Moon: Release and Resolve

The moon starts to decrease from full to dark again during this phase. After the highs of the full moon, it can feel like an anticlimax, but it is perhaps the most important phase because it shines moonlight on the importance of completion and letting go of what is no longer needed, including any beliefs about dreaming that are blocking your chances of recall. What you do during this phase can determine the success of the other three phases. 'Balance' and 'harmony' are keywords during this time. It is a time to exhale, release, resolve, heal and daydream about your night vision.

BIGGER DREAM TIPS

- Gazing at the moon before you go to sleep may help you connect to your intuition and encourage your intuition to flourish in your dreams. If you can see the moon from your window at night, gently focus on it for a few minutes. If you can't see it or if the moon is dark, find a picture or photo to reflect on, or visualize the moon in your mind's eye.
- Lunar energy is said to be at its most potent when the moon is full, though there is no proof of this. It is also said that drinking moon water, which is simply tap water left overnight under the light of the full moon, boosts your intuition – the intuition you want to speak loud and clear in your dreams. Might be worth a moon shot!
- Consider placing a small moonstone crystal beside your bed to boost dream recall. In my humble opinion the power is in you, not the crystal, but crystals do have certain energies, and if you believe they work, that might have a placebo effect. Other dream-boosting crystals include amethyst, rose quartz, aventurine, lapis lazuli and citrine.

PRESENTIMENT

In addition to getting your daily moon fix, or if lunar living isn't for you, there are other ways to ignite your intuition. Perhaps the simplest and most direct is to pay attention to physical signs. Intuition often speaks first through your body when you are awake,[2] so pay attention to messages from your body. Notice any gut feelings, butterflies in the stomach, loud heartbeats, bitter tastes in the mouth and so on, and acknowledge why those feelings have arisen.

MOOD SCAN

Intuition touches your heart rather than your mind, so tune into your moods regularly. Like your dreams, your emotions have so much to share with you.

Moods are a natural part of being human. There are no 'right' or 'wrong' moods – and, like your thoughts, just because you think or feel something doesn't mean you *are* that thought or feeling, simply that it is passing through you. But recognizing and understanding your feelings can help you work out what causes or triggers them, how you tend to behave when you experience them and, over time, how you can manage them better. Most moods pass within a day and you can track them using well-being tools and apps like Headspace, or you can simply write down how you feel in a daily journal. Don't try to explain them – sometimes we feel things that just don't make sense – just write down whatever feels authentic. Remember that nobody is going to see this journal but you. You don't need to follow any structure. Your feelings and your dreams don't!

IN THEIR SHOES

Seeing things from another person's perspective increases empathy and the ability to lose yourself from time to time. Identifying with how someone or something must feel enhances intuition. For instance, the next time you find yourself in an argument or getting angry when you talk to someone, pause for a moment, take a deep breath and consider the impact of your words or actions on the person you are talking to and why they may be feeling the way they do. It's a real game-changer.

In much the same way, you can also consider yourself better in hindsight. Reflect on a past mistake to see if there were any warning signs from your intuition that you missed. Identifying why you didn't notice intuitive nudges can help you to avoid missing them again.

'Aha!' Moments

There's been a surge of interest in intuition and its ability to triumph over logic in recent years. The popularity of TV shows such as *Sherlock, House* and *Medium* is a case in point.

Science,[3] and even the US military,[4] has also been very busy proving that intuition is a real super or, as the Navy describes it, 'Spidey' sense.

From Einstein to Oprah, highly creative people who credit their intuition as the source of their success pay close attention to their dreams. Did you know that scientist James Watson figured out the design of DNA, the chemical basis of all life, from a dream he had of a spiral staircase? And that this became the catalyst for his discovery of the double helix?

Your Dream Works: *Spidey Sense*

WHAT YOU'VE LEARNED: The more you flex your intuition muscle in waking life, the more confident it will feel to express itself clearly and expressively in your dreams. Tuning into the moon's phases is a simple and easy way to go within and fine-tune your intuitive powers.

TAKE NOTE: For one lunar month (or more), write down how being aware of the moon's phases impacts you. See if you notice patterns and if moonlight is directly inspiring or influencing your dreams.

9

A Quiet Place

There is a strong association between regular meditation and a rich and rewarding dream life.[5] There is a sound reason for this. Meditation is a proven[6] concentration-boosting technique that helps you observe your thoughts, feelings and surroundings without judgement. You simply notice whatever passes through your mind. You detach and don't judge or fear whatever your mind wants to reveal to you, just as you aspire to do whenever you 'wake up' in a dream.

In this way, daily meditation 'trains' you to separate your mind from your body and become more observant of yourself and your reality when you are awake, so it's something your dreaming mind won't have a problem doing when you are fast asleep. It helps you tune directly into your intuition and grasp the might of your own mind. Indeed, deciding whether your current awareness is real or not is how all lucid dreaming begins.

But you can't become lucid in your dreams if you aren't first fully aware in your waking life. And one of the best ways to become more aware is to take regular time out to calm your mind.

FIND YOUR WAY

TAKE TWO

One of the simplest ways to electrify your life and your dreams is to set aside two minutes every day of dedicated 'quiet time'.

I'm using the words 'quiet time' here rather than 'meditation' or 'mindfulness', as both of these 'm' words sometimes have associations that aren't helpful. You might even be tempted to switch off because they sound too time-consuming or complicated. Or perhaps you've tried them and found they aren't for you. Not surprisingly, as high-energy, creative people often don't want to be told to slow down. However, if you want to have spectacular dreams that you can potentially wake up in, setting aside just two minutes to become more and more 'you' – the infinite, intuitive, creative you who never sleeps and remains wide awake in your dreams – is a true dream-igniting catalyst. And it only takes two minutes.

- Find somewhere peaceful where you can sit comfortably, with your hands gently resting on your lap and your back straight.
- Set a timer for two minutes.
- Either close your eyes completely or half-close them and look downwards.

- Tell yourself that you will be still.

- Just be still and breathe.

- You may notice that many thoughts compete for your attention during this short time. Don't interact with them or push them aside, just let them flow past you like a leaf on a stream you are sitting beside.

- When the timer goes off, open your eyes and congratulate yourself on completing two minutes of quiet time.

You might notice with welcome gratitude how refreshing it feels to have taken some time out from the constant demands of your attention-seeking thoughts. This is because this highly effective technique has reminded you that your thoughts do not define or own you. It's also refreshing because we spend so much of our waking time over-thinking. And in all that mental rush we barely pay attention to who we truly are.

Just taking two minutes out of your day to slow right down and find calm encourages you to be more appreciative, observant and conscious of both yourself and your present reality.

BIGGER DREAM TIPS

- If you think you can't find two minutes of quiet time in your busy day, perhaps this is a sign that your life is getting overcrowded. If you want to have lucid dreams, the place to start might be clearing your diary.
- If you find this two-minute exercise helpful, you may want to repeat it twice a day or extend your two minutes. There are benefits to prolonging your quiet time, but don't fall into the trap of thinking that the longer you meditate, the more progress you are going to make. You need to go for quality not quantity with your quiet time.
- To further leave your thoughts behind it can sometimes help to focus your attention entirely on your breathing. When you close your eyes, breathe in very slowly through your nose and then, when your lungs are full, exhale slowly and completely through your mouth. Notice how it feels when air enters your nostrils and sails down your throat and into your lungs. Concentrate on the sensations when you exhale. Notice that every act of inhaling and exhaling is different. No two breaths are the same.
- If closing your eyes makes you feel sleepy and this is blocking your progress, it might be time to check in again with #4, *REM Expansion* (*see page 29*), and pay attention to your sleep hygiene. Also, be sure not to perform this exercise lying down.

ONE STEP AT A TIME

Another highly recommended exercise that complements daily meditation is to take a mindful walk. Mindfulness isn't quite the same as meditation, but it is closely related and equally calming, inspiring and beneficial for your waking and dream life. The difference is that when you meditate, you calm and clear your mind by observing your thoughts and feelings, and mindfulness is more about being fully present in the moment and aware of your surroundings as well as your thoughts, feelings and movements.

Again, mindfulness is simple, and you don't need to go on extensive training courses to learn how to be mindful or to walk mindfully. You can do this whenever you are walking, whether indoors or outdoors.

- Dedicate two minutes of your walking time to thinking about nothing but your own steps.
- Direct all your focus on your walking, not just your feet as they hit the ground or floor, but also your legs as they move you forwards one step at a time, your arms as they swing, your head as it leads the way.
- If other thoughts crowd in (and trust me, they will), just let them pass by.

- Next, expand your full attention from the act of walking itself to include your surroundings. What do you see and hear? What are your senses sharing with you?

- Take in all those tiny details all around you that you would normally miss.

- Look at the world around you like a detective hunting for clues.

If you want to add an extra-special dimension to this and can find somewhere clean and safe, you can do your mindful walking barefoot on the earth, grass or sand. This is a therapeutic exercise called 'earthing'. Focus deeply on the feeling of the soil, mud, soft grass or sand beneath your naked feet as you walk and your connection to the ground.

Meditate to Graduate

Aside from its ability to calm your mind, ignite your intuition and influence your dreams, meditation has also been shown to boost mood, mind and physical health.[7] There is even a movement to get it taught in schools, as one study showed that students who meditated regularly were more likely to graduate.[8] And research on meditating monks suggests that daily meditation can literally change the structure of your brain, thickening key areas of the cortex concerned with attention and concentration or self-reflection.[9]

Your Dream Works: *'A Quiet Place'*

WHAT YOU'VE LEARNED: Taking a few minutes of quiet time to observe your thoughts gives you a golden opportunity to train yourself to be mindful or conscious when you are wide awake, so that when you dream, awareness becomes more automatic to you.

TAKE NOTE: When you have completed your quiet time, write down how it made you feel. Did dream memories or intuitive insights surface? Or did you just feel calm, clear-eyed and ready to dream and explore with deeper appreciation of your life?

#10

Deep Unwind

The focus remains firmly on your waking awareness today. But this time you are going to carefully observe how your body and mind slow down or relax prior to going to sleep. In short, you are going to find out how it *feels* to drift off and leave your physical senses and your body behind.

Chances are you haven't really thought about how you fall asleep before. It is something that just happens when you are tired. But becoming conscious of what you experience when you are deeply relaxed is key to understanding what happens when you actually transition from waking awareness to the wacky and wonderful world of your dreams. It proves to you what science confirms: that it *is* possible for a part of you to remain conscious when you are asleep.[10] And the more awareness and belief you have that there is a *you* who exists separately from your body and mind, the more likely you are to recall your dreams and, in due course, know when you are dreaming.

FIND YOUR WAY

TOTAL RELAXATION

Performing a progressive relaxation exercise is a simple and effective way to notice exactly how you feel before you dream. Research shows that progressive muscle relaxation really can help you to de-stress physically, mentally and emotionally.[11] Indeed, regular progressive relaxation is often recommended by health professionals for well-being.

The best time to perform this deep relaxation exercise is when you feel tired, just before you fall asleep. But to increase your chances of success, it's best to do a trial run first during the day. The reason for this is that if you first try to perform this technique when your head hits the pillow, you may automatically fall asleep before you have a chance to initiate conscious awareness of that falling-asleep process. So, practise first before you try it at bedtime.

- Find somewhere where you won't be disturbed and where you can lie down comfortably.
- If it's daytime, draw the curtains to shut out the light so it's as dark as possible.
- Set a timer for ten minutes.

- Count backwards from ten down to one.
- Then breathe in and clench your hands for a few seconds.
- Breathe out and suddenly (not gradually) relax your hands entirely.
- Notice how at peace your hands feel.
- Repeat the tensing and relaxation steps, working through your whole body in the following order:

  arms (flex them)
  shoulders (shrug them)
  forehead (wrinkle or frown)
  eyes (close them as tightly as you can)
  jaws (smile as broadly as you can)
  neck (touch your chin to your neck)
  chest (breathe in deeply)
  back (arch it a little)
  buttocks (clench them)
  thighs (clench them together)
  lower legs (point your toes)

- Now that every part of your body is fully relaxed, keep still and feel any physical sensations fade away.

- It's time now to turn inward and employ the meditation skills you learned previously. Observe whatever thoughts or feelings enter your mind. Notice any images that dart around behind your eyes.

- Separate yourself from your thoughts and feelings until your body feels weightless and disappears and you are all that there is.

- When your alarm goes off, gently re-enter your body.

- Take your time switching back to your conscious reality.

- When you are ready to see the world around you again, open your eyes and have a big stretch.

Once you have practised this relaxation exercise, go to bed around fifteen minutes before you normally do and give it a try as you melt into sleep. Your goal is to unwind physically but remain alert mentally. This physically relaxed but mentally alert state is the entry point for the lucid dream state, and the more you practise reaching it when you are awake, the more natural it will feel when you are asleep. Remember there is continuity[12] between your waking and sleeping life, and that continuity is *you*.

You might find that when you perform this exercise, not only do you start to see mental images (visualization), but sometimes you can see yourself lying on your bed. This can be described as an out-of-body experience. It's something that you may also experience fleetingly when you are fully absorbed in a task. For instance, musicians say that it can happen when they are performing. But don't let the term 'out-of-body' alarm you. You aren't leaving your body, you are just exploring the infinite potential of your consciousness while you are in a state of deep relaxation.

TOTAL RELAXATION (MINI VERSION)

If you are low on time, you can try out this great short-cut.

- Simply breathe in, and as you do so, tense your entire body for a few seconds.
- Exhale deeply and let all the tension go.
- Feel your body sink into the bed and become heavy.
- Let everything go and focus on your hopes of better dreams.

BIGGER DREAM TIPS

- The muscle relaxation order I have suggested above is considered optimum for deep relaxation, so you might want to read it out and record it on your phone. Or you can easily find free progressive muscle relaxation audio recordings online.

- If coughing, sneezing or clearing your throat interrupt your relaxation, have a glass of water and start again or return to it another time.
- If you find it hard to relax physically, this exercise can prove challenging. Stretching gently before you lie down can help, as can listening to some soothing music, breathing deeply or writing down any anxieties in a journal. Other proven ways to chill out include massage, yoga, a warm bath, going for a walk or drinking herbal tea or warm milk. Find out what works best for you.
- If your thoughts are too invasive, try to imagine yourself chilling on a beach, in a meadow or any place that calms you. Add in as much detail as you can, so that in your mind's eye it feels real. Incorporating a winding path that you wander happily down can also help.

Nidra Style

This technique draws much of its inspiration from an ancient Indian technique found in the Vedic and Upanishad scriptures called Yoga Nidra, also known as yogic sleep, in which a person is given a set of verbal instructions to guide them into a state of deep physical relaxation, while remaining mentally alert. It has the same goal of calming the mind as meditation but differs in that, although the focus is on the inner world, the sense of hearing remains, so that the person can hear the instructions. Yoga Nidra is regarded as one of the deepest possible states of relaxation while still maintaining full mental consciousness. The aim is to achieve conscious awareness of the deep sleep state.

Yoga Nidra has spread outside India and is now used all over the world for stress reduction.[13] The US army has utilized it successfully to help soldiers recover from PTSD. It is certainly a technique you might want to experiment with on your inner journey. But be aware that when it comes to consciously knowing how you relax and fall asleep, it's always better to discover how that feels for yourself.

Your Dream Works: *Deep Unwind*

WHAT YOU'VE LEARNED: Given the continuity[14] between being mindful in your waking life and being aware of how you fall asleep, this exercise will, in time, help you stay awake mentally as you watch your physical awareness fade away.

TAKE NOTE: Once you become familiar with how relaxing physically and mentally before falling asleep happens for you, write down in a notebook or journal exactly what happens to your body and mind. How do you experience each stage in that drifting away process?

#11

'Is This a Dream?'

You are now just over the halfway point on this thrilling journey into your dreams. It's high time to dive into the eye of the storm or the beating heart of the swirling insights that are waiting to reveal themselves to you in your dreams. You are going to choose your 'Am I dreaming?' reality check.

'I do not know whether I was then a person dreaming I was a butterfly, or whether I am now a butterfly dreaming I am a person.'

Zhuangzi, *The Butterfly as Companion: Meditations on the First Three Chapters of the Chuang-Tzu*

I never tire of referencing this timeless quote whenever I talk or write about lucid dreaming. And it is particularly apt to place it here in the heart of this book because it encapsulates the essence of reality checking. It is a tried-and-tested lucid dreaming tool that, like all the others you are learning, is so natural and effortless to do.

Everything you have learned up to this point has encouraged you to become more mindful and self-reflective. The more self-reflective you are, the more you understand that you – not other people or situations – are the creator or director of your life. In much the same way, you are the creator or director of your dreams.

Now you are going to build an unbreakable bridge between your waking mindfulness and your dreaming awareness or lucidity. Mindfulness and lucid dreaming aren't really separate concepts, even though they are often presented that way. Mindfulness is lucid dreaming's soulmate. Both processes need, want and sustain each other.

FIND YOUR WAY

QUESTION EVERYTHING!

You can literally make anything you repeatedly do during the day your reality check – opening a door, getting dressed, having a cup of tea, watching TV, walking, and so on. Just choose something in your daily routine that you normally do more than once and elevate it to reality-checker status. Choose something that feels natural to you. It doesn't matter what the actual reality check is, or whether it is inspired by something you see, do, think or feel. But when you do it, ask yourself, 'Is this my real life? Is this a dream? If it's a dream, can I fly?' In real life, of course, you'll keep your feet firmly on the ground, but if it's a dream, you'll soar away.

Then ask yourself how you know you are not dreaming, and don't stop asking till you are absolutely sure you are awake.

You could also do your reality check whenever you get a text or alert on your phone. Read that text or alert once and then reread it. In real life, the text or alert will be unchanged, but in a dream, there's no telling what else might be unfolding.

Want to go further with your reality checks? You can also try the following methods.

SLIPPING THROUGH YOUR FINGERS

This is a very popular exercise, perhaps because it is a physical reality check rather than a mental one. It's something you can easily *do*. It's also great fun. I love it because you can do it anytime as a break from mental reality checks.

- Take a moment to push the index finger of one hand into the palm of the other hand.
- As you do this, fully expect your finger to go through your palm and at the same time ask yourself if you are in a dream.
- If you fully expect your finger to do this and you *are* dreaming, it will happen. *Voilà*! You know you're dreaming! Of course, if it doesn't happen, you *aren't* dreaming.

- You can also count your fingers every day on the hour. As you count them, fully expect to have more than ten fingers and ask yourself if you are dreaming. In a dream, those fingers will multiply fast if you ask them to. In real life, you are stuck with your basic ten.

CHARMED

You may prefer to do your reality checks using a charm or something small that you carry around with you all the time. Ideal choices are a ring, a die, a pocket-sized moonstone or rose quartz crystal, a coin, a toy, or any small object. What is important is that you can always carry it with you. Your dreams mirror your daily life, so chances are, if you keep using your charm as your reality check, it will eventually make a cameo appearance in your dreams.

- Every time you want to do a reality check, take your 'charm' out and focus all your attention on it.

- Get to know it – how it looks and feels – in intimate detail.

- Inspect it from every angle until you have noticed everything about it.

- When it appears in a dream, it won't be quite the same as it is in real life. When you spot that difference, you'll know it's a dream.

BIGGER DREAM TIPS

- Once you have chosen your reality check, check your reality daily, for two weeks minimum.
- Repetition is key. Ten times a day is optimum, but you can still achieve results if you only do it once or twice a day.
- You can help to discipline yourself by setting a reminder on your phone each hour or by putting a sticky note on something you look at every day, like a desk or mirror.
- Reality checks aren't effective if done in isolation, so you need to use them in combination with the other practices in this book, especially those in Week Three.
- If talking to yourself to verify your reality is starting to feel uncomfortably close to crazy, take stock for a minute. Although you may not realize it, you use self-talk all the time and many of your thoughts are probably far crazier than asking yourself if you are dreaming.

Dream–Waking-life Checker

At this point in your life you have already had countless dreams, whether you have recalled them clearly or not. What you need now is a radical shake-up, a powerful association to trigger the realization that you are dreaming. You can purchase (as I did) a spinning top and go full *Inception* style, but you don't really need any kind of charm. You can find something in your waking life that speaks to you. Or, to keep it really simple, just ask yourself right now: 'Is this a dream?' That's your initial dream checkpoint done already.

Your Dream Works: *'Is This a Dream?'*

WHAT YOU'VE LEARNED: Verifying whether you are awake or dreaming during the day, using a reality check or charm of your choice, can naturally filter into your dreams, offering you a chance to wake up in them.

TAKE NOTE: Once you have chosen your reality check, note down how often you have carried it out during the day. You may also want to experiment with different reality checks to see if some feel more natural than others and therefore increase the likelihood of you practising them more often.

#12

Daydream Believer

Have you experienced a fleeting moment of awareness or clarity in your dreams yet?

The definition of a lucid dream is 'knowing that you are dreaming while you are dreaming'. But there is a scale or range[15] of how you may experience awareness while dreaming, from a vague knowing, to some ability to control, to detailed recall, to stunningly vivid. There is also a perfectly valid lucid dream state you can enter which is woefully neglected or totally ignored by the dreaming community. Practice #3, *Imaginators* (*see page 22*), hinted at this transformative dream state by encouraging you to embrace the potential of visualization. It's high time now to come out and talk loud and proud about your natural-born ability to dream with your eyes wide open.

Daydreaming, contrary to what you may have been conditioned to believe, isn't a waste of time. It has incorrectly been associated with laziness, boredom and inattentiveness, and you may even have been reprimanded for doing it at school, but your brain actually remains active when you daydream. Indeed, research has shown that when your brain is 'idle', it is still operating at a very high level,[16] much higher than originally thought. Used in moderation, mind wandering[17] has been shown to be a highly productive use of your time. Of course it is. It's on the spectrum of dreaming and therefore isn't meaningless. It has all the intuition, creativity and problem-solving benefits of dreaming.

So, if you want to give your dreaming mind some much-needed attention and reassurance, give yourself permission to daydream. Remember when you were a child and you dreamed of being an astronaut and/or flew to the stars and back in your daydreams? Time to reconnect with that inner child and let your infinite dreams return. Daydreaming is a natural, fun and seriously under-valued way to ignite your intuition and creativity and train yourself to dream bigger and better.

FIND YOUR WAY

SAIL AWAY

You can let your mind wander anytime you like, whether alone or in a group, but daydreaming when you are alone is more productive. There is also no risk of interruption, and you can sail away and lose yourself in your inner world.

It's best to avoid the period directly after lunch to do this exercise, though, as you might feel too sleepy. The ideal time would be mid-morning or mid-afternoon. And if there is an option to do it outdoors in a natural setting, go for it. Being in nature connects you to your intuition and infinite creativity more quickly, as a part of you instinctively feels part of something so much bigger than yourself.

- Find a quiet place where you are unlikely to be disturbed.
- Switch your phone to silent and set a timer for five minutes.
- Sit down comfortably and close your eyes.
- Take a few deep breaths and imagine you are breathing in calmness and exhaling tension.
- Next, visualize a light shining out of your head.
- Open your eyes.
- With your eyes wide open, recall an image or fleeting scene from an intriguing dream you've had recently (this should be a dream you had when asleep).
- If nothing comes to mind, visualize a scene from your favourite movie or book and place yourself right in that scene.
- You are now both the director and the actor in the movie of your daydreams. It is your dream boat. Sail away in a direction your dreams take you, however strange.

- When the timer goes off, visualize a director's clipboard closing the scene. It's a wrap.

- Stand up, have a good stretch and a glass of water to ground yourself and settle back into the reality of your life.

Don't be shocked if you feel a little hesitant to return. You've just been to an inner universe of infinite possibility. Things are different there.

It's possible to use daydreaming to improve any skill or to rehearse any situation you feel uncomfortable or unsure about, for example giving a presentation. Of course, as you will discover next week, lucid dreaming also offers you this fantastic opportunity. But for now, your daydreams can be a great dress rehearsal for that exciting possibility. Simply visualize and then daydream about what you want to learn or improve, or how you want a certain situation to develop, then let your dreaming mind do the rest.

CLOUD WATCHING

If creating mental pictures doesn't come naturally to you, you can use a trigger for your daydreaming. One technique that has always worked well for me is cloud watching.

- Find a place outside where you can sit or, better still, lie down on your back comfortably and safely.

- Gaze up – don't stare – at the clouds above you. Be sure not to look directly at the sun.

- Just watch the clouds as they float by.

- What shapes do you see? What do they make you think of? Let your mind roam where it will.

- You can do this indoors, too, by looking out of a window.

- You can even add in some daydreaming at night by doing a spot of stargazing. The clouds and stars, like your dreams, are always there to inspire you.

BIGGER DREAM TIPS

- Too busy? Some of the highest-achievers in the world, with packed diaries and lives, still stress the importance of taking time out to contemplate. Steve Jobs, the co-founder of Apple, very famously valued solitude as it gave him time to daydream.
- There can be a stigma around being happy in your own company or needing to spend time alone. So, remember

that being introverted doesn't mean you are anti-social, it just means you are selective in the company you keep and highly value your inner world. Don't resist any tendencies towards introversion you may have. Instead, embrace them. Sensitive is the new strong, and introverts can be compassionate, sociable and extremely powerful in their own right.

- If neither of these techniques work for you, don't put pressure on yourself. Your life may be busy or stressful, or you may be repressing your creativity due to past trauma or personal reasons. Make self-care and stress management a priority, talk to friends, family or a counsellor if you need to, and try this technique again when you feel rested and recharged.

Absent-minded Professors

There is fascinating new research to suggest that people who daydream may actually be smarter and more creative than people who don't.[18] This is intriguing, as daydreaming is typically associated with a wandering, undisciplined mind but it seems the opposite may be true. Daydreamers have active brains – in fact, so active they can't stop their minds wandering.

Your Dream Works: *Daydream Believer*

WHAT YOU'VE LEARNED: When you daydream and let your mind sail away, you aren't wasting your time, you're simply indulging in some dreaming during the day. Your daydreams are powerful.

TAKE NOTE: Write down the story of your daydream, or if there was no story as such, what you daydreamed about and how it made you feel. Compare it with the stories, content and emotions of your night-time dreams. How similar or different are they? Your dreams reflect your inner world – who you truly are – so if there are striking differences, consider how much you are utilizing your creativity in your waking life.

#13

Tuning In

Sounds played at certain frequencies have been shown to help tune up our thinking and boost our concentration and focus. They can also help us relax. But are certain sounds good for improving dream recall and triggering lucid dreaming?

Yes. Today's exercise will introduce you to the sound benefits of tuning in.

Ever since research indicated that regularly listening to Mozart could boost children's brain power, educators have linked listening to sound with improved study and problem-solving.[19] Indeed, the 'Mozart effect' has stimulated a music-in-education industry. Experts believe listening to music 'wakes up' both the logical and creative parts of the brain at the same time. The more logical, rational part of your brain works on pattern recognition, while the creative, intuitive part is free to dream. Activities that use your brain's full capacity in this way are believed to boost your thinking skills and your creativity.

Whether you buy into the Mozart effect or not, there's no doubt that sound can have a transformative impact. Like dreams, sounds can express and reveal things that words can't. Both can speed you up and slow you right down. Both can inspire, heal and stimulate your imagination. Both can bring clarity and carry you far, far away.

As you journey deeper into the fantastical world of your dreams, you can't have a better friend, mentor, companion and champion accompanying you than sound, with all its power and joy.

FIND YOUR WAY

BINAURAL BEATS

Binaural beats are two separate frequencies that are played at the same time, but enter each ear individually. Your brain, however, processes and blends them into a single frequency. To benefit your dreaming, and potentially trigger episodes of lucid dreaming, the frequency (Hz) needs to be between 4Hz and 8Hz, as that induces the appropriate theta brainwave state linked to deep meditation (*see page 46*). The sounds you hear range from humming to rushing sounds and to help you along they can sometimes be augmented by natural sounds like running water, waves or falling rain. Regularly listening to binaural beats, also known as brainwave entrainment, can also help induce the wake–sleep meditative state so conducive to night visions.[20]

There are many free binaural beat tracks online and on YouTube, or you can download a brainwave entrainment (aka brainwave synchronization) app to your phone. A good free one is Brainwaves Binaural Beats, which has sounds specifically designed to induce lucid dreaming.

When you first listen to binaural beats, they may sound strange. It is important to realize that you are listening to sounds created by sound engineers to guide your awareness with specific frequencies. Don't expect to hear music or a melody and don't over-think it. Just get comfortable and let the beats do their work. If you still find that the sounds annoy you, then this technique isn't right for you. The aim is to relax, not tense up.

For this exercise, you will need a pair of headphones.

- Lie in bed with the lights off, preferably at the end of the day.

- Simply listen to your chosen binaural beats and enjoy the feeling of deep relaxation and inner harmony the sound ignites in you.

- Within the first few minutes you are likely to feel noticeably calmer.

- Within ten minutes you are likely to be more deeply relaxed.

- Let yourself drift off.

Binaural beats aren't necessarily going to kick-start a lucid dream. They can do, but they are more likely to lull you into a calm and timeless zone, which is very helpful for creating self-awareness when you dream. In other words, they increase the likelihood of lucid dreaming, not necessarily on the night you listen to them but over the coming nights. You increase the likelihood of going automatically from wakefulness into a deep state of relaxation.

If you don't want to fall asleep wearing headphones, you can still listen for ten minutes or so and then take them off before dozing off. Alternatively, you can set aside ten minutes or so mid-morning or afternoon to listen. It's best to do this alone and in a quiet place, but it isn't essential. Just put your headphones on and let your mind flow with the harmonizing sounds you hear.

LULLABY

Soothing melodic music is proven to calm and inspire the brain[21] and it's a great alternative if you decide binaural beats aren't for you or you want a break from them. In the Resources (*see page 193*), you'll find the link to a half-hour 'Dream Notes' classical piano lullaby – a gift exclusively curated for you.

MAKE MUSIC

Whatever age you are, you can light up your brain and potentially inspire sweet dreams by learning an instrument.[22] But if you don't want to, there's another way you can make sweet music. You can sing in a choir, into your hairbrush or in the shower or car. Or you can simply hum to bring a little extra harmony into your life. Toning can also help fine-tune your brain. Chanting *Ahhhh* and

Ommm (*Aum*) immediately feels harmonizing and relaxing. Try some toning for a few minutes each day or before you go to bed.

SOUND APPS

You can download a range of sound apps, such as Slumber, Noisli and Calm, designed to help you relax and fall into dreamy sleep, and many of them are entirely free. These apps will typically feature nature sounds, such as waterfalls, wind, rain, etc., or ambient sounds played in a loop. Experiment until you find the sound track to ignite your dreams.

Along the way you may also encounter a range of cutting-edge lucid dreaming apps which use the power of sound to induce lucid dreaming. For example, the Binaural Beats therapy app has sections with sounds specifically designed to boost lucid dreaming. Although I have yet to discover my ideal lucid dreaming app, this doesn't mean they won't work for you. Everyone is unique.

As well as utilizing sound therapy, some of the lucid dreaming apps can be of practical help too – for example, ones such as Lucid Dreamer that have a built-in reality checker to remind you every hour or so to perform your reality checks, or ones like Dream Journal Ultimate that encourage you to record your dreams in a way that can help you identify patterns and themes. Again, experiment to see if any resonate with or help you. Don't stress if they don't. Lucid dreaming apps aren't for everyone.

Genius Dreams

Albert Einstein is recognized as one of the greatest minds ever to grace the planet and, as you'll recall, a dream actually inspired his theory of relativity. Yet there was no sign of his genius when he was young. His performance at school was so poor that his parents were told he was 'too stupid to learn' and it would be a waste of time and energy to invest any further in his education. His school therefore advised his parents to remove him and find him a manual labour job. But his mother ignored the advice and bought him a violin instead. He loved playing it and practised until he was highly skilled, often improvising for hours when he needed to solve a complex problem. Could making music have been key to unlocking his genius and stimulating his visionary dreams?

BIGGER DREAM TIPS

- You may enjoy listening to soothing music before bedtime, and white noise is a deeply relaxing alternative you may want to consider.
- Many of us eject music completely from our lives as we get older. And that is a great loss for our brain, our life and our dreams, because music inspires all three. If listening to music doesn't feel natural or appropriate anymore, think

'young' and welcome music back into your life. Ditching conventional ideas about what is appropriate or not is also fuel for your dreaming mind.

- There are always windows of time in the day for listening to soothing sounds. You only need a few minutes. Go to bed a few minutes earlier than usual to make sure you fall asleep listening to something relaxing.

Your Dream Work: *Tuning In*

WHAT YOU'VE LEARNED: A little music every day can boost your creativity, but listening to certain sounds – in particular binaural beats – before you go to sleep may help you relax and dream bigger and better.

TAKE NOTE: As you incorporate more music and the power of sound into your daily routine, write down which sounds and pieces prove more likely to trigger sweet dreams. Over time, you can create your own dream-inducing sound and music playlist.

#14

The Album

Dream recall is an act of self-care and self-awareness. It is caring deeply about yourself and your inner life and noticing how much your dreams and your waking life reflect and sustain each other. The next transformative stage is, of course, becoming lucid in a dream – and next week will offer you a stunning crash course in that. But, as you've seen, it just isn't going to happen if your dream recall isn't firmly established first.

One of the most valuable and proven[23] ways to cement your connection with your dreaming mind and increase your chance of dream recall and dream lucidity is to have a dedicated dream journal.

I deliberately waited until now before encouraging you to commit yourself to a dream journal. I am hopeful that the previous thirteen practices have seriously ignited your dream recall, so you have lots to write about whenever you wake up. But if you still feel you are seeing through a glass darkly, this practice might just be the spark, the catalyst you need. If dream journaling feels new to you, think of it in the same way as you would your photo album. You store those vivid images for future reference because they are special memories. They all mean something to you. Your dreams are special memories to you, too, and this is your way of remembering and keeping them all in one place – your own private collection.

FIND YOUR WAY

WRITE AWAY

Putting your dream down on paper should take no more than a few minutes. It's best to focus on the major themes and feelings rather than every detail. You do need to get into the habit of writing down your dreams every morning, though, and every time you wake up from a nap or a sleep. Commit to it. Think of it as your sacred dream ritual. The important thing is to establish the habit of writing down something on waking.

- Every night place a piece of blank paper and a pen beside your bed.
- If you know it's going to be dark when you wake up in the morning, make sure you have a nightlight that you can use when you write.
- As you put the piece of paper by your bedside, tell yourself that you are going to have amazing dream recall in the morning.

- When you wake up in the morning – hopefully naturally rather than with a stressful alarm clock – don't blink, just keep still.
- If no feelings or images come to mind, ask your dreaming mind to send you some.
- Ask it where you were, what you were doing and what you encountered.
- Check in with your body and how it feels, as sometimes dream memories linger there.
- As soon as any messages or symbols or colours come through, sit up, stay calm and write them down.
- Write in the present tense, as this helps keep the dreams fresh, for example 'I am flying'.
- Just write down anything that comes to mind – colours, images, impressions, sounds, symbols, people, things, animals, places, and so on.
- Don't try to make your dream tell a story or make any sense, and forget about correct grammar or beautiful handwriting.

- Pay attention to the *feelings* the dream inspired.

- When you have written down everything you can recall, turn the piece of paper over and have a go at drawing something you saw or felt in your dream.

- When you have finished, make a note of the time and date.

- Leave the interpretation for now and get going with your day.

It helps to have some distance from your dream, so you can be objective when you come to look at it again. You can reflect on its meaning later, perhaps in the evening. Having said that, you may find, as I do, that random dream images can pop into your mind at any time during the day, so carry a notepad around with you and write them down.

Your Dream Journal

A blank piece of paper beside your bed is a visual reminder that the blank sheet needs to be written on. It's a method that works well for me, but of course over time you're going to have stacks of paper. I use A4 with holes punched in it, and when I have written up my dream, I put the paper in a folder. But you may prefer to purchase a journal or notebook, because it is a tidier way to keep a record of your dreams. If you do buy a journal to write your dreams in, make sure it's one that is a pleasure to write in. And use a pen that writes smoothly and feels good to hold.

TALK IT OUT

If writing isn't for you, you can also record your dreams on your phone, type them up or download a dream journal app, such as DreamKeeper or Awoken. The pros of these kinds of apps are that as well as recording your dreams, they allow you to immediately search for recurring themes and signs without looking through handwritten notes. It's not ideal to use your phone first thing in the morning, but if that's what suits you best, it's right for you and your dreams.

BIGGER DREAM TIPS

- If there is nothing to write or talk about when you wake up, make a note of that and ask your dreaming mind to talk to you next time you dream. It's normal not to remember dreams every morning, especially if your waking life is super busy, but don't give up on your dreams. Persistence is everything.
- If too many images make writing down your dreams time-consuming and laborious, then just choose one or two

dream memories and focus on those. Celebrate the fact that your dreaming mind has so much to share.

- Reliving your nightmares can be upsetting, but it is important to understand that the best way to deal with them is to work with them. Try to understand what they want you to know and regard their nocturnal messages as a self-help tool. They are not attacking you. They are an SOS.

Your Dream Works: *The Dream Album*

WHAT YOU'VE LEARNED: There is no escaping the fact that keeping a dream journal every day is essential for your dream recall. You may also find that simply enjoying keeping a record of your dreams triggers unexpected lucidity.

TAKE NOTE: Think of your dream journal as an album of your soul. Write in it every day, whether you recall your dreams or not. Respect every single snapshot as a powerful message to your dreaming mind that you truly want to listen to what it has to say. And whenever your morning dream recall is clear, be sure to reflect on the evening before. What did you eat? What did you do, watch, read, think, feel? Something captured your dreaming mind's attention or increased the likelihood of better recall. Through trial and error, over time, you can work out what your dream combination is.

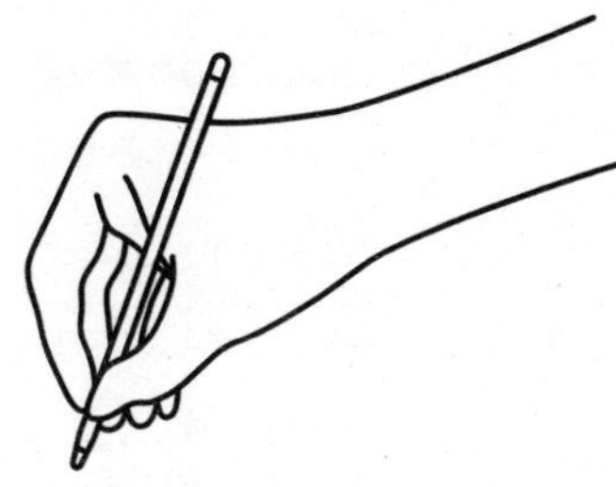

YOUR WEEK TWO DREAMER'S CHECKPOINT

Congratulations on completing Week Two. The fact that you have reached this point shows you are now in a deeply committed relationship with your dreaming mind and your night vision is taking note!

To get the most out of Week Three, you need not only to notice your dreams and value what they want to tell you, but to be truly, madly and deeply in love with all your dreams. But before you plunge head first into experimenting with some full-blown lucid dreaming tools, you might want to pause a little now to reinforce fully what you have learned so far, especially if dream recall and clarity is still an issue. So here's a brief overview of what you've done this week to help you keep track.

#8: SPIDEY SENSE

- ○ Get your Moon Fix
- ○ Lunar Cycles
- ○ Presentiment
- ○ Mood Scan
- ○ In their Shoes

#9: A QUIET PLACE

- ○ Take Two
- ○ One Step at a Time

#10: DEEP UNWIND

- ○ Total Relaxation
- ○ Total Relaxation (mini version)

#11: 'IS THIS A DREAM?'

- ○ Question Everything!
- ○ Slipping through your Fingers
- ○ Charmed

#12: DAYDREAM BELIEVER

- ○ Sail Away
- ○ Cloud Watching

#13: TUNING IN

- ○ Binaural Beats
- ○ Lullaby
- ○ Make Music
- ○ Sound Apps

#14: THE ALBUM

- ○ Write Away
- ○ Talk It Out

Dream Catcher

SEVEN WAYS TO 'WAKE UP' IN YOUR DREAMS

'The future belongs to those who believe in the beauty of their dreams.'
Eleanor Roosevelt

A gentle reminder before you turn the page that by now your dream recall should be convincing most mornings or, at the very least, a few times a week. I just can't stress how important clear recall is for the success of this week's final, and arguably most potent, lucid dreaming practices. If you still have to catch up with your dream recall, I urge you to read these next pages, but *not* to attempt the exercises until your dream memories are clearly there. Reading about these techniques may well trigger something magical, but if you try them without having established regular dream recall, you are likely to get frustrated. The practices so far have all been lovingly designed to boost your dream recall and awareness, so be sure to keep repeating them. And don't forget to celebrate every dream memory you have from now on, as a sign of your progress and growing awareness.

Everything you have done up to this moment has been essential practice. You now know that your dreams reflect your waking life, so ask yourself whether you are truly 'awake' when your eyes are open. Are you someone who sleepwalks through life without asking questions of yourself or are you an alert truth-seeker who looks beneath the surface of things?

It's high time for you to start waking up not just in your dreams but also in your daily life. The next practice will set the scene by introducing you to simple ways to immediately decode the meaning of your dreams.

The remaining six techniques, in stark contrast to the previous fifteen, aren't designed for daily use. They should be performed no more than once or twice a week, or as and when you feel ready to do them.

As exciting as it all is when you start waking up in your dreams, please pace yourself. Your dreams will vanish without a trace whenever you try to force them or you neglect the creative potential hidden in your non-lucid dreams and your life.

Remember, your waking activities, thoughts and feelings feed your dreams, and every dream, whether it's lucid or not, is a priceless message that deserves your love and respect.

So, the best advice for you right now is to keep calm, count your fingers, carry on breathing deeply, living fully and dreaming ever more clearly.

#15

Decoding Time

Once you start regularly recalling your dreams, you are going to be eager to understand their meaning. What exactly are your dreams trying to tell you? Because they rarely make any sense at all, this is where dream-blocking disillusionment can set in.

This practice will help sweep aside any misunderstandings you may have about the meaning of your dreams. It will offer you simple but highly effective dream-decoding tools that you can apply to all your dreams. It is also very helpful for inducing lucidity, because it underlines the fact that every dream is rich in meaning and a powerful self-help tool.

You understand on a deep level that your dreams are not random and are loaded with hidden potential and creativity just waiting for you to explore. Every time you decode a dream, you remind yourself that your dreams are an untapped resource. They matter.

FIND YOUR WAY

REVISIT YOUR DREAMS

As already mentioned, it's not advisable to try and decode your dreams on waking. Far better to write them down in your journal and then return to them with fresh perspective later in the day.

When you're ready to revisit your dreams, find somewhere quiet where you can reflect and, slowly and carefully, read what you've written. Study your dream drawing if you did this. You may also want to read your dream thoughts out loud if you are alone. The ideal time to do your decoding is just before you go to bed, as it invites your dreaming mind to reveal more information to you.

As you read, be aware that your dreams don't make sense because they are speaking in the picture language of symbols and metaphor, not the language of waking reality. Symbols say so much more than words ever can, and are great teachers in personal growth. For example, a rainbow can symbolize hope. There can be endless interpretations and each time you revisit symbols new perspectives and associations may come. So, your dreams aren't a literal replica of your life but a symbolic, poetic representation of them. In ancient times, humanity had a natural understanding of the power of pictures and symbols to reveal profound truth, but one of the casualties of modern life is the loss of our ability to see beyond the superficial, the literal meaning. So, don't be surprised if learning to decode your dream symbols is much easier than you thought it would be. This is because you are not really *learning*, you are *remembering*.

Be aware that symbols often have a conventional and universal meaning. My *Dream Dictionary from A to Z* outlines those for you. These are associations that are generally accepted or widespread in many cultures. For example, if you dream of a butterfly, this is a symbol of transformation or change. However, in addition to these universal meanings, there are your personal associations, which are crucial to your interpretation. For example, if you love dogs, the universal meaning of companionship and loyalty applies, but if you fear dogs, you need to add in your personal feelings of being threatened if a dog appears in your dreams.

DREAM-DECODING FUNDAMENTALS

Here are five dream-decoding fundamentals to help you get started with your own dream decoding. Simply apply them to everything you recall from your dreams and you'll become an accomplished dream oracle for yourself (and perhaps even others if they ask you to help them understand a dream).

- **LOGIC FIRST:** The majority of dreams are symbolic, but sometimes they can be obvious. So, always rule out the literal or logical explanation first. If you dream, for example, of your teeth or those of a loved one falling out, do you or they need to visit the dentist? If, however, a dream feels irrational and bears no relation to the present moment – your dreams are always about your present circumstances, even if they use symbols from your past to comment on your present – then it's time to reflect more deeply on it and decode its symbolism.

- **YOU AND ONLY YOU:** When you are dreaming, every symbol and scenario can represent something about you or your waking life. It really is like stepping into a hall of mirrors. So, when you dream about other people and things – for example, if you dream of your best friend becoming a snake ask yourself, are they to be entirely trusted, but also ask yourself what aspect of yourself they represent that you need to acknowledge, face, express, understand, heal or integrate. The great majority of the time you will find that your dream is all about *you* and only you.

- **YOUR ROLE:** Establish who you were in your dream. Were you powerful or vulnerable? How did you think and feel? How did you react? What did you recognize about yourself? Or were you doing something unexpected? If you were observing yourself, why were you detached? (If you don't like your usual role in your dreams, know that you can change it.)

- **LOCATION, LOCATION, LOCATION:** The setting of your dream will often be a clue about its meaning. For example, if you are back at school, what is the lesson here? If you are in a supermarket, what are you searching for? After considering where you are, think about what you are doing there. In dreams, as in life, actions speak louder than words. Colours that you see in dreams also have messages. Do some research on their significance. For example, red is the colour of action, yellow of intellect, orange of creativity; green is associated with growth, blue with calmness, purple with spirituality, and so on. And if weather plays a part – for example, if it is sunny or stormy – that can offer you important insights about your state of mind.

- **MOTION:** Movement of any kind in a dream is symbolic of your current progress or path through life. Are you flying or falling? Are you walking without a care or sinking into quicksand? Are you chasing someone or something or are they chasing you? If you are in a vehicle, are you the driver or a passenger? Do you know which direction you are heading in or is the vehicle out of control? How fast or how slowly are you going?

Your dreaming mind often resorts to recurring symbols, people, colours and feelings when it is really trying to drive a point home and get you to pay attention to certain issues. These signs may also help you recognize when you are dreaming, because the more aware you are of them, the sooner you can identify that you are dreaming. Think carefully about these repeating signs. Your dreaming mind could have chosen any symbol from the infinite number out there, but it is shining the spotlight on this one for a reason. You need to find out why. That's what is so awesome about working with your dreams – you realize how endlessly interesting you are!

Bear in mind that your familiar dream signs are likely to keep reappearing until you fully understand their meaning. And if you do have a recurring nightmare, stay calm. Your dreaming mind is using tough love to make a very important point. As soon as you understand the message, the nightmares will end.

DREAM THEMES

Here are some common recurring dream themes and their meanings. Bear in mind that certain dream themes appear at different stages of life, with children and teenagers often having dreams that turn the spotlight on discovering possibilities within them, whereas the dreams of adults focus more on the themes of choice or perspective, and older adults tend to have dreams that are about finding meaning.

- **FALLING:** This is the most commonly reported dream. It can feel alarming and may be a sign you are feeling unsupported or out of control in your waking life. Pay attention to how you feel when you fall, because if you enjoy it, then you are going with the flow.

- **FLYING:** If you are flying in a dream, do you need to rise above your situation and see the bigger picture?

BEING CHASED: What do you want to avoid or what are you not dealing with in waking life? You need to face whatever it is before it catches up with you. Dreams of being late are related and suggest being unprepared or missing out.

DEATH: In dreams, death means change. Something is ending or needs to die within you or in a relationship for there to be a new beginning. It is not a precognition if you or someone you love dies in a dream, just a sign that the relationship is changing in some way, or needs to. If there is a murder in a dream, this is a sign of change being forced upon you.

BIRTH: In much the same way, dreams of giving birth or being pregnant aren't precognitions, but symbols of new beginnings and ideas about to be born.

LOSING TEETH: Is this fear of how you look or appear to others or fear of ageing? It can also suggest that you are feeling angry about something or, if your mouth is full of gum, chewing over a problem. Teeth dreams are also linked to communication or how you express yourself. Do you need to pay more attention to your words? Do they match your actions?

MALFUNCTIONING PHONES: Dreams that feature malfunctioning phones may also be asking you to pay more attention to your words and communications.

- **A HOUSE:** According to Jung, the father of dream interpretation, houses in dreams are mansions of the soul, with the various rooms representing aspects of yourself. If you discover a secret unused room or find money or a hidden treasure, it suggests hidden potential or that you need to deal with what you have repressed. And if you dream of burglars or someone trying to break into your home, then something unusual is challenging you in waking life.

- **WATER:** This is a universal symbol of emotion. So, if you are drowning, do you feel overwhelmed? Notice if the water is clear and calm or turbulent. If it is raining in your dream or there is a tidal wave or storm, again link your interpretation to an emotional outpouring of some kind.

- **NATURAL OR MAN-MADE DISASTER:** If the world is ending in your dream due to a natural or man-made disaster, this is a clear sign of an unexpected change in your waking life and feeling helpless in the face of it. Your dreaming mind wants you to focus on the promise of a new beginning after your world has been shaken to the core.

- **LOST:** Have you lost touch with a part of yourself or are you losing a sense of direction in your waking life? Closely related to this are dreams where you are on stage and forget your lines or are trying to do something that can't be done. This means you are feeling vulnerable or frustrated in some way in your waking life.

- **TRANSPORT:** Notice any cars or other modes of transport in your dreams, because they represent the direction your life is headed in. Is the vehicle out of control? Who is in the driver's seat? If it isn't you, why are you a passenger?

- **MOVEMENT:** In much the same way, notice how you move in a dream, as this links to your current progress in waking life and how you feel about it. Are you walking without a care in the world, struggling uphill or stuck in the mud?

- **NAKED:** If you are naked in a dream or need to use the bathroom in public, this suggests that you feel exposed and vulnerable in some way. Pay attention to how you feel in the dream, because if it doesn't bother you, then you may want to reveal something about yourself in your waking life.

- **EXAMS:** What is testing you in waking life? You may feel anxious about how you are performing. (Interestingly, people who dream about exams tend to do better in them.)

- **SEX:** Your dream lover represents an aspect of yourself that you need to acknowledge or integrate for your personal growth.

BIGGER DREAM TIPS

- You'll know if you've understood the meaning of a dream because you'll have an 'Aha!' moment of sudden clarity.
- If there is no illumination, ask your dreaming mind to give you more clarity the next time you dream. The correct interpretation will also feel energizing rather than draining, positive rather than negative. Indeed, you may prefer to set aside time to interpret your dreams every few days or once a week rather than every day, because, like a Netflix show, dreams often need a series to make their mark.
- If you want something sensational to read a yearly or monthly review of your dreams is enlightening. You'll see how your dreams and waking life are connected: how dreams offer out of the box perspectives to help you evolve.
- Be aware that your dreams will often tell you what you don't know or need to know about yourself. Expect the unexpected.
- Sometimes your dreaming mind has a sense of humour and will use puns to get a point across. For example, if you dream you are checking your mail and are a woman looking for a male life partner.

All about You

Seek out that iconic scene in the movie *Inception* where everyone in the dream stops to stare at the dreamer. This really is how the vast majority of your dreams work. You are

dreaming about aspects of yourself and everything you experience in your dream is about *you. You* create the world of your dreams. Once you truly understand this, your dream decoding can really take flight!

ASSOCIATION

Association is a useful dream-decoding technique you may want to experiment with. When you recall a dream symbol, write it down and then immediately write down the first thing that comes to mind. If nothing comes to mind, focus on the emotion the dream symbol evokes in you and see what associations emerge from there.

Your Dream Works: *Decoding Time*

WHAT YOU'VE LEARNED: Almost all your dreams are personal and should be interpreted symbolically and psychologically, not literally.

TAKE NOTE: Write down absolutely everything that your dreams ignite within you. Pay attention to every symbol, story and feeling. Nothing in a dream is trivial. There's no telling what astonishingly creative connections decoding your night visions can inspire in the coming days, months and years.

#16

Inception

The waking life–dream connection doesn't go only in one direction, but feeds back in a loop: your dreams don't just mirror you and your waking life, you can influence your dreams.[1] *Dream incubation* is a technique you can use to encourage a specific dream topic, either for fun or because you want to solve a problem. For example, if you are nervous about an upcoming exam, you can incubate a confidence-boosting dream in which you ace the exam! The sleep temples of ancient Greece, which were healing sanctuaries for people to be prescribed spiritual or medicinal cures for whatever ailed them, practised dream incubation, and it was brought to public attention and made famous over 2,000 years later in the film *Inception*. Many indigenous shamanistic cultures swear by it, and 'dreaming on it' is something many scientists, artists and inventors have done remarkably successfully.

This practice will introduce you to techniques that can help you incubate a lucid dream. All the techniques rely on a combination of the power of your intention and the power of your memory. But I'm not talking about retrospective memory of something that happened in the past, I'm talking about future memory or prospective memory. This is remembering to recall something you intend to do at a future time. It's whenever you tell yourself something such as 'Next time I book cinema tickets, I'll book VIP seats.'

Sometimes we write down the things we must do in the future to remind ourselves of them. But most of the time we just keep them stored in our mind until the time comes to recall and do them. Today you are going to add lucid dreaming to your essential do-in-the-future list.

During the day, remind yourself as often as you can that you are going to dream vividly the next time you dream. If you are a forgetful person, then do what you would do if it was really important for you to remember it: write it on a sticky note and put it on your mirror or desk, or set an alarm reminder on your phone. What you are doing here is strengthening your intention to have a lucid dream by working on your instinctive ability to recall and do something that is important you remember to do.

Then, when it comes to bedtime, whisper out loud the following words to yourself:

'The next time I dream,
I will know that I am dreaming.'

Now you are ready to experiment with three closely related lucid dream incubation techniques that can, if used with caution and calmness, actually work.[2] They are the Mnemonic Induction to Lucid Dreaming (MILD) technique, the Wake Up, Back to Bed technique (WBTB) and the Finger-Induced Lucid Dream technique (FILD).

Don't let these technical-sounding titles faze you. The techniques may sound complicated, but none of them is.

FIND YOUR WAY

THE MILD TECHNIQUE

This is the heart of dream researcher Stephen LaBerge's MILD technique to induce a lucid dream[3] by creating a prospective memory intention to remember you are dreaming by repeating phrases like 'Next time I dream, I will remember it is a dream.'

- If you do wake up in the night and recall a dream, stay in bed and write it down on a blank piece of paper or in your dream journal.

- Memorize those dream details.

- Then lie down and go back to sleep, visualizing the dream in vivid detail.

- If you want to rescript the dream, decide how to change it.

- See your rescripted dream playing out behind your closed eyes.

- Select a reality-check moment and imagine yourself performing it in your dream.

- As you step more deeply and completely into the memories of your dream, repeat your mantra: 'Next time I dream, I will remember it is a dream.'

- Continue until you fall asleep.

Be aware that the MILD technique can take a week or so to yield results. In the meantime, just write down all your dream memories, even if they aren't giving you what you think you are looking for. You may not notice any answers or connections right away, but may do so in hindsight. Remember that dreams have so much they want to share with you that sometimes they need several nights to make their point. Carry on dreaming!

THE WAKE UP, BACK TO BED TECHNIQUE

The Wake Up, Back to Bed (WBTB) lucid dream incubation technique is one that you should use with caution, as it involves disrupting your sleep schedule. Best to do it only occasionally or when you are on holiday. It's not designed for daily or long-term use. With this warning in mind, though, it may be something you want to experiment with.

- Make sure you go to bed before 11 p.m.
- Set a nice soothing alarm for 3 or 4 a.m., which is when you are most likely to be in REM sleep (if you work night shifts, adjust accordingly, or simply set your alarm a few hours before it normally goes off).
- When the alarm goes off, sit up and write down any dreams you can remember.
- Visit the bathroom if you have to or have a glass of water. The aim is to stay awake doing something calm and/or dream-focused for around five to ten minutes. You want your brain engaged but your body sleepy. It's a great time to read your dream journal.
- Next, set your alarm for when you need to wake up and go back to bed. When in bed, replay any dream memories you have in great detail. Visualize yourself waking up in that dream.
- Repeat your desire to lucid dream as you drift off to sleep.

The theory is that waking early means the deep sleep, non-REM cycles will be largely behind you and your brain will be eager to push you quickly into the REM stage when you go back to sleep to ensure you get it. Remember, your brain needs plenty of REM sleep for healthy function, and the REM stage is when you dream the most.

PLAY THE FILD

The way FILD (Finger-Induced Lucid Dreaming) works is that the finger movement keeps your mind conscious as you fall asleep. This lucid dream incubation technique is ideal for when you are really sleepy or when you wake up in the night.

- While you're lying in bed, gently wiggle your middle and first fingers or any two fingers you choose.
- Start with a big two-finger wiggle, as if typing on a keyboard.
- Wiggle them less and less until they are barely moving.
- Stay focused on that small movement in your fingers to help keep your brain responsive to them while the rest of your body drifts off to sleep.

- Combine this slight finger movement with your desire-to-lucid-dream mantra until you fall asleep and dream.

MILD, WBTB and FILD are lucid dream incubation techniques, but you can simply use dream incubation by itself to ask your dreaming mind to offer you insights on issues in your waking life. In this way, you can become your own dream oracle! For example, you may want insight or a fresh perspective on a relationship or work issue, or perhaps you wish to meet a departed loved one in your dreams. Write down your request before you go to sleep, think about it and ask for dream insight. Chances[4] are your dream, whether lucid or not, will comment on the issue in some way. Make sure your question is clear, and really feel it when you ask it. Your dreaming mind doesn't respond to vagueness, so know what you want and feel confident about asking for it.

None of these techniques requires a huge effort. They are fuelled by your desire to dream. But if you find them tedious or energy-sapping, simply *stop*. Lucid dreaming is a fun self-help tool. You get to explore your own creativity, discover deeper meaning and remove toxic patterns in your life. So, always approach your dream work in a spirit of respectful enjoyment. If you get tense or stressed about it or disappointed with the results, you won't progress. If this is ever the case, make 'I love my dreams', 'I love dreaming' or 'Dreams are fun' your new mantra.

BIGGER DREAM TIPS

- Sometimes it's good to place a visual symbol of your intention to lucid dream beside your bed, so you can see it when you fall asleep and wake up, as this can help focus and empower your intention. A moonstone or other small crystal can be a great focal point for your dream incubation.
- Heavy sleeper? Lucid dreaming does tend to occur in the lighter REM phase of sleep prior to waking, rather than the deeper phases of sleep earlier in the night. If you are one of those people who sleeps like a log, the best advice is to focus on those mini-awakenings, especially in the morning. Be sure to change your sleeping position – say, from your side to your back – and to repeat your lucid dreaming mantra then.
- Having a particular sleeping position that you associate with lucid dreaming can also be a helpful trigger for it.

Dream Devices

As lucid dreaming is pleasurable and can be used to successfully treat nightmares and stress disorders, a number of technology companies have developed portable lucid dreaming devices, sleeping masks and even headsets for use by the general public.[5] These devices include: Dreamlight, Nova Dreamer, Aura, Remee, REM Dreamer, ZMax, iBand, LucidCatcher and Aladdin. Of them, ZMax seems to be generating a lot of endorsements from dream researchers, but in the world of cutting-edge technology there is constant change and evolution.

These devices work by detecting REM and then using visual, auditory and/or other sensory stimuli to alert dreamers they are dreaming without waking them up. I've tried a few and they've had little noticeable effect on me, but I live in hope. Don't let my experience put you off experimenting. However, I have found that the techniques suggested in this book have been enough. Indeed, I feel the do-it-yourself approach is a more powerful way to wake up your dreaming mind, because relying on technology or something external to do the work for you doesn't set the right dream tone. However, I always keep an open mind, and if you decide to explore the lucid dreaming technology out there, let me know if you come across any app or device that works reliably for you. (Details of how to get in touch with me can be found on page 193.)

Your Dream Works: *Inception*

WHAT YOU'VE LEARNED: There are certain tried-and-tested dream incubation techniques, such as MILD, that can help you programme your mind to send you dreams big enough to wake up in. Experiment with them to see if any of them hold the key to your dreams.

TAKE NOTE: Please remember to keep writing down your dreams, especially when you have experimented with a specific technique. In the morning, note down which technique you used alongside your dream experience. Your dream journal or record is your case file; the evidence you gather together there will help you decide which techniques are most effective for you.

#17

Go WILD

This technique is called Wake-Induced Lucid Dreaming, or WILD. Like the three techniques of the last practice, it has sound research backing[6] and yet another catchy acronym, which is something the lucid dreaming community seems to love. Although it remains controversial, if you follow the safety guidelines below it might just be the red pill method you need right now (referencing that iconic *Matrix* movie scene where Neo has a choice between taking the blue pill and remaining unaware or the red pill and seeing things as they really are).

When you use the WILD technique, what you are aiming to do is remain conscious or awake as you fall asleep and begin to dream. You have already been gently preparing yourself for this with the meditation and deep relaxation suggestions in Week Two (*see pages 73 and 80*). Time to rev things up now. But it's going to take a little effort and practise on your part to achieve success.

FIND YOUR WAY

NIGHT OWL

There are a number of versions of WILD out there, most, if not all, inspired by the 'godfather of lucid dreaming', Stephen LaBerge. What I'm offering below is a version of WILD that delivers for me, but, as lucid dreaming is a celebration of your uniqueness, it's best to experiment to find the variation that speaks to you personally.

- Just as with the MILD technique, aim to go to bed before 11 p.m. and set your alarm for five or six hours later (adjust accordingly if you work night shifts).

- When your alarm sounds, get up and stay awake for around twenty to thirty minutes.

- During this 'night owl' time you should preferably read or do something related to your dream work, but it's not essential. You can do the ironing if you like. The important thing is that the activity is calming and doesn't make you too wide awake.

- Go back to bed, lie back and keep still.

- As you lie there, feel your body melting into the bed.

- Let go of physical sensations and calm your mind using the techniques you learned last week.

- You are now entering what is known as the *hypnagogic* state between waking and sleeping. You may see colours or shifting shapes and faces, or hear echoes in your mind. Observe all this as you would your thoughts, with calm coolness.

- Keep your entire focus on your inner world. Let it totally eclipse your outside world.

- Enjoy the fun TV show behind your eyes. Remember, your dreams reflect your feelings and amplify them. You are the driver here.

Be aware that when you first practise this technique, you are likely to find yourself in a dream that looks and feels very much like your own bedroom, because that was the last thing you saw before you fell asleep. Eventually you may be able to direct your mind to other scenes, but don't rush things. Rejoice in this newfound awareness of your dream bedroom. This is the stuff lucid dreams are made of.

COUNTING IN YOUR SLEEP

This is a version of WILD which can be very effective and which will disturb your sleep less. In this version, to help maintain awareness, you consciously count, question your reality and cycle through your senses as you journey from waking in the night to dreaming.

- When you wake up after around five hours' sleep, get up, write in your dream journal and focus your full intention on your desire to wake up in your dreams.
- After ten minutes or so, go back to bed, lie down and close your eyes.
- As soon as your eyes are closed, question your state of consciousness as you count down to a dream:

  'One: Is this a dream?'
  'Two: Am I in my dream?'
  'Three: Am I dreaming?'
  'Four: Am I lucid now?'
  And so on, repeating the same or similar.

For the first twenty or so questions, your answer is likely to be: 'No, I'm awake.' But after that you may find that you are less certain, and as your count edges towards the fifties there's a good chance you are conscious in a dream. Best to stop the count once you get above 100, because if you aren't awake in your dream by then, chances are this isn't working for you.

CYCLING IN YOUR SLEEP

Instead of counting down to a dream, you can try another variation, which involves cycling through the senses of sight, hearing and touch as you fall asleep:

- When you get back into bed after your period of 'night owl' waking (*see above*), with your eyes closed, 'see' what is behind your eyelids for a few moments.
- Then shift your focus to any external or internal sounds you hear.
- Next, cycle your focus to your body and how the bedsheets feel or what the air feels like on your forehead.
- Cycle through these three stages – seeing, hearing, feeling – five times.
- Then go through them again, but this time spend longer in each.

Both counting and cycling as you fall asleep are designed to hack your brain and give it no choice but to dream consciously.

BIGGER DREAM TIPS

- WILD does require you to adjust your regular sleep schedule, so the ideal time to do it is over the weekend or when you are on holiday or not working, driving, studying or operating machinery. Please don't go overboard with this technique, as one of the best ways to lucid dream is to enjoy your sleep and wake refreshed. You are strongly advised not to do it more than twice a month. On the other days, undertake the same steps but at your proper bedtime, rather than waking up to do them at 3 or 4 a.m. You can also apply them if you decide to take an afternoon nap.
- Waking up in the early hours of the morning takes a brave heart, so it's understandable that you may not want to try this technique if you feel anxious, sensitive or vulnerable getting up alone in the darkness. Having said that, once you do it the first time, you may understand why so many highly creative people get up in the early hours. The peace and quiet is exquisite and highly conducive to creative thinking. You may even find that when your alarm goes off at 3 a.m., your mind is crowded with spectacular dream memories and sudden illuminations. Don't hesitate to write them all down. They might just change your life for the better.

Brain Hack

Waking before your regular rising time panics your brain into thinking it is going to be deprived of REM sleep, which it needs to function healthily. As soon as you go back to sleep, it therefore flings you back into the REM stage. And if you do WILD several times over the coming months, the shock of the technique might condition your conscious mind into becoming more alert in the early hours of the morning. So even when you aren't going WILD, if you have done it a few times previously, you may still automatically lucid dream.

Your Dream Works: *Go WILD*

WHAT YOU'VE LEARNED: Experimenting with WILD, or variations of it that help you fall asleep and dream consciously, can dramatically increase your chances of becoming aware that you are dreaming *while* you are dreaming.

TAKE NOTE: Write down your experience of WILD in your dream journal. In particular, see if you can identify and describe in detail how it felt when you knew you were at that exact moment when your thoughts transformed into dreams.

#18

Thresholds

Now it's time to focus more fully on the magical threshold of dreaming, those twilight moments before you enter your wonderful dream world, and how they can be used to guide your mind and body into a state perfect for lucid dreaming. As your bodily awareness fades and reality feels warped, these threshold moments can feel trippy or as if you're hallucinating. And perhaps, understanding more fully what happens to our mind just before we fall asleep may one day help solve the mystery of human consciousness.

FIND YOUR WAY

SLEEP PARALYSIS

During your WILD technique, you may (or may not) become aware of what is known as sleep paralysis. This is that feeling you may get when you are about to fall asleep or when you have just woken up and, try as you might, you can't move your limbs. It's your body's way of stopping you from physically acting out your dreams. This is especially important for lucid dreamers, as it stops them leaping out of bed in their sleep and trying to actually fly. It is something that happens every night, although most of the time you have no conscious awareness of it. The scientific term for it is 'REM atonia'.[7]

It's great to become intimately familiar with how REM atonia feels, so you know how to react when it next happens, because it is often a prelude or entry point to the awareness that you are dreaming. If you make friends with your REM atonia, you can let it take you by the hand and lead you right into a lucid dream.

Most people will experience REM atonia at least once. It can happen to anyone, but it is more common if your sleep schedule isn't regular. When you first experience it, your initial reaction may be distress, but these steps can help you to embrace this unique sensation.

- REM atonia happens on the threshold of sleep. Try to stay calm and don't resist the sinking feeling. REM atonia is your friend. It won't and can't harm you in any way.

- Don't try to move your arms or legs or head or any part of your body.

- Take the attention away from your body to your inner world – your mind.

- Enjoy this transition from waking to sleeping or sleeping to waking and tell yourself over and over again, 'This is a dream.'

- If doubts creep in, smile at them.
- Visualize something or somewhere soothing that has a natural rhythm, like a pendulum or a sandy beach with waves dancing on the shore.
- Allow your attention to focus on the pendulum as it consistently and calmly crosses from side to side or on the dancing waves as they gently lap backwards and forwards. Let the rhythm you decide on draw or pull you into your dream.
- Just relax and allow your floating mind to take you surfing right into your dreams.

REM atonia can be a cause of fear and, as your dreams respond to your feelings and thoughts, wherever there is fear, nightmares are possible. Remind yourself you don't have to be afraid. You can transform a potential nightmare into a potential lucid dream (*see page* 160).

MEET THE 'H' TEAM

Hypnagogia (hypnagogic: from the Greek *hupnos*, 'sleep', and *agōgos*, 'leading', so 'leading to sleep') is a close companion of REM atonia. Both are signs you are on the threshold of a dream. Hypnagogia is what happens to you mentally rather than physically when you are falling asleep. Have you ever closed your eyes after looking through a window flooded with bright light, or at a candle, and seen patterns and lights dancing on the backs of your eyelids? That's sort of what hypnagogia is like.

Just like REM atonia, not everyone will experience awareness of hypnagogia, but if you remain aware and enjoy the mysterious firework display hypnagogia brings rather than panic, it might whisk you right away into a lucid dream. If it happens to you, just allow the images to unfold. Then, see if you can exert some influence over the shifting patterns by bending them into images you want to see. Paint the scene behind your eyes. Put in vivid, realistic details and when the dreamscape you have visualized feels alive and real, see yourself in it.

It's not just when you are drifting off to sleep that you can superimpose your creativity on what unfolds behind your eyes. You can also do it immediately on waking, in a similar borderland state called hypnopompia (hypnopompic: from the Greek *hupnos*, 'sleep', and *pompe*, 'sending away', so 'sending away sleep'). There's a lot of attention paid to the hypnagogic state, but not enough to its twin, the hypnopompic. The two 'H' states are similar, but have a slightly different feel, with hypnopompia more likely to recreate scenes from your real life than its arguably more creative twin, hypnagogia. But both states can induce a lucid dream, so if you wake up early, keep your eyes closed and see if episodes of lucidity follow.

You'll know when you enter either 'H' state because you'll find your thoughts becoming slower and calmer, you might see shifting patterns, colours or faces behind your closed eyes, and waking reality will drift away...

BIGGER DREAM TIPS

- Once you have a growing awareness of being in the hypnagogic state, you can try switching your mental focus to physical sensations and your breath. You will still see hypnagogic imagery, but keep your awareness gently on your body and your breath. Don't consciously scan your body, just let your body draw your attention to it.
- Awareness of these threshold dream states can help induce lucidity, but it's certainly not essential. If you aren't experiencing them then perhaps this isn't your optimum way to lucid dreaming.
- Be aware that you are far more likely to experience hypnagogia than REM atonia, but if you don't think you experience that dreamy state either, the likely reason for it is that you aren't going to bed tired enough. You are far more likely to become aware of dream-like states when you are feeling really sleepy, both mentally and physically.
- Taking a daily nap for around twenty minutes is considered to be a very good thing by health experts, as it can recharge and refresh both your body and your mind. Indeed, successful companies like Google have reserved napping places for their staff. A nap is also something simple you

can do on occasion to encourage lucid dreaming, because when you nap, you tend to skip the delta-wave, deep-sleep stage and enter lucid dreaming-friendly REM sleep right away.

- If experimenting with any of these techniques makes you feel too tired, *stop*. The whole point of lucid dreaming isn't to deplete your energy but to enhance it. Revisit Weeks One and Two until you feel recharged and refreshed and ready to dream again.
- If you are concerned that these techniques are making you lose touch with reality, *stop*. Take all the time out you need to honestly reflect on why you are drawn to lucid dreaming and what you want to gain from it before experimenting any further. Your dreams will always want you to fall in love with yourself and your waking life, not distance yourself from it.

A Dream Within a Dream

This happens when you get up and start your day as usual and then you wake up for real and realize you were dreaming the first time around. It's not the same as REM atonia, but you are more likely to experience it if you do also experience sleep paralysis. It can feel unnerving, but the advice is to make friends with this 'false awakening'. Every morning when you wake up, it's a good idea to question whether you are dreaming or not. The first time you check your watch or clock, switch on the lights or look in your mirror, ask yourself if this is a dream. If it's a false awakening, there will be something odd about it. For example, the lights may not work or you may not be able to see your reflection in the bathroom mirror. Perform your reality checks and you never know – your false awakening could become your first or next lucid dream.

Your Dream Works: *Thresholds*

WHAT YOU'VE LEARNED: Making friends with and working with sleep atonia and the borderline sleeping and waking states can help induce a lucid dream.

TAKE NOTE: Make a note of the date and time you are aware of sleep atonia or the 'H' teams to see if there is a connection between what you do during the day and the likelihood of having that awareness. If you don't become aware of these states, don't worry. Your dreams know the best way to reach you. Trust them.

#19

Don't Let your Dream Collapse

There is something wonderfully inviting about a blank page or intentional silence, isn't there? You feel compelled to question, wonder, reflect. Your instinct is to fill in the space or the silence with your own creativity. There's potential and possibility there, just as in a lucid dream.

The final three practices in this book just can't follow the same 'how to' format as the previous eighteen. Why? Unlike the previous exercises, they operate under the assumption that you are now getting at least a glimpse of the lucid dream experience. The blank page, the silence, the shift in tone are deliberate and designed to zoom all your attention onto this breakthrough moment in your growing awareness of your own infinite potential as a human being and a human dreaming. However, if you aren't there yet, don't feel disheartened. You're working at your own pace, and lucidity will come when you're ready. Do read this section, though, as you may find reading about keeping being in a lucid dream is just the trigger you need.

From now on, I simply can't presume to define or determine your lucid dreaming world and the infinite wonders awaiting you there. The time for following or copying is well and truly over for you now. You are in your own dream world, and everything that happens there will be utterly unique, just like the utterly unique miracle of DNA you are. All I can do moving forward is humbly offer some 'travel tips' for your nocturnal adventures.

FALLING APART

If you've ever woken up in a dream, chances are you've almost immediately woken up. That's a start. The next step is to learn how to stay in a lucid dream.

First things first, though. If you've experienced this 'dream collapse', don't let your natural frustration demotivate you. You're bound to feel disappointed with yourself for letting this opportunity slip away, but congratulate yourself instead. You've woken up in a dream. You've finally done it! You've created a bridge to the other side of yourself. You're completing yourself. Congratulations!

It is exciting, isn't it? When you first wake up in a dream, your immediate response is likely to be intense excitement. It's amazing, but you can't quite believe or trust it, and the surprise instantly wakes you up. (Dream collapse is depicted brilliantly in *Inception* in all those incredible scenes when everything comes crashing down around the dreamer like an avalanche.)

When this happens to you – and it has happened to me many times – smile at yourself. Your excitement has simply shown your dreaming mind what a big deal waking up in your dreams is for you. Your dreaming mind will be flattered and, trust me, you'll soon be offered another opportunity.

YOU'LL MEET AGAIN

Once you have had that first moment of lucidity and collapse, expect a few more false starts. Again, when this happens, there's no reason to get angry with yourself. In the beginning it is very typical to only have fleeting moments of awareness in a dream. See every one of these fleeting moments as taking you one step closer to a more sustained lucid dreaming experience. Your mind needs time to get used to your brave new dreaming world.

And getting lucid is really just the beginning. Staying with your dream is the true skill to learn from now on. So, how can you do that?

The next time you become aware in a dream, remember *you* are in charge of your reaction. Just as in your waking life, you are in charge of what you think and feel. So, keep your euphoria in check. Cultivate serenity.

Once you are calm, look around and observe every aspect of your dream, including yourself. Perform several reality checks to be absolutely sure you are in a dream. Study your hands closely. Is this a dream? Repeated reality checks will keep your dream stable, and the longer you remain in the dream each time, the easier it will be for you to remember to stay calm whenever you become lucid. Keep telling yourself that it is a lucid dream and you are cool with that. Tell yourself to remain calm and stay with your dream.

Other ways to help prolong the experience are to rub or clap your hands, spin around or fall backwards in your dream. All these movements can stimulate your conscious mind and you may well find your dream becoming more vivid.

TRUST IN YOURSELF

Perhaps one of the most potent ways to avoid dream collapse is to remind yourself that everything in a dream is your own creation. If there are things you fear there, they are simply hidden aspects of yourself that you need to understand better.

Once you really grasp that your dreams aren't external or separate from you but belong utterly and completely to you, you can extend a hand of friendship to them. The more positive you feel about them, the more they are going to reward you. In short, knowing you are dreaming about yourself and that your mind has created everything in your dreams will really reassure you. And the more you trust in your dreams and treat everything you encounter with respect and compassion, the less likely your dreams are to frighten you or collapse around you.

STAY LUCID

To stay lucid in a dream, keep sharpening your observation skills in waking life. The more you get used to staying alert, the easier it is to avoid dream collapse.

You may also find that after a tantalizing moment of lucidity, you find the dream so absorbing that you forget you are dreaming. Your dreaming mind has grown used to you not being aware of it, so you do need to constantly tell yourself you *are* still dreaming. If you don't retain this lucid awareness, your dream will return to being non-lucid.

Alternatively, you may find that you know you are dreaming, but when you ask your dream to help you do something extraordinary, such as fly, you can't.

To help you maintain the awareness that you are dreaming *and* believe you can do the impossible in that dream, you need to return to those reality checks. When an impossible thing happens, this is your reminder that you are dreaming and the impossible is possible. You can fly if you want to. Just have supreme confidence in yourself and in the magic of your dreams.

A DREAMY NOTE

If you do have a lucid dream, be sure to treat yourself a little the following day. Perhaps you could gift yourself a small moonstone crystal or indulgent massage. It doesn't matter what it is, just mark the occasion. Celebrate your achievements!

And be sure to clearly mark on a blank page or in your dream journal the date and time of your first (or next) lucid dream and carry on recording all the other lucid dreams you have after that. You might want to use a different coloured pen or journal to record your lucid dreaming journey. Make it stand out from your non-lucid dreams as a permanent record of meeting and holding onto yourself in your dreams and just how extraordinarily transformative, meaningful and healing the experience can be.

Your Dream Works: *Don't Let your Dream Collapse*

WHAT YOU'VE LEARNED: Waking up in a dream can trigger dream collapse. However, there are ways to stop your dream falling apart.

TAKE NOTE: Keep track of what techniques work best to keep you awake in a lucid dream. This is going to be trial and error. Find out what works best for you. Be patient with yourself and your dreams.

#20

Shadow Facts

We need to talk more about nightmares – those terrifying dreams we all have from time to time.

If you do have a nightmare, be aware that the intense fear you experience can be turned to your advantage. The shock and surprise put your dreaming mind on high alert, increasing your awareness of having an extremely bizarre dream and the likelihood of you becoming lucid. When you experience a frightening dream, being aware that it isn't real and you are the source of its power can result in a seismic psychological shift which can help you resolve issues holding you back in waking life.

Shadow Facts will help you understand how your shadow side is being presented to you in your lucid dreams, so you can use that transformative insight to stop running from those night monsters and confront them. Just as a fever is unpleasant but a positive sign that your immune system is helping you heal from infection, aim to think of nightmares as the dreaming mind's immune response to help you heal from waking anxiety and stress.

INTO YOUR SHADOWS

According to Jungian psychology, the shadow side of your personality is the aspect of yourself that you feel unable to express honestly, because it is something you feel uncomfortable with or don't want to admit to in your waking life. The shadow side isn't evil. It is simply what you and/or others deem unacceptable. For example, your anger or jealousy. It is hidden, but in a nightmare it screams out for your attention by revealing things about yourself that you've repressed or don't want to deal with.

A nightmare isn't some dark or separate external event that happens to you. It *is* you. It reveals what is hidden in your life, what you need to face and manage for your personal growth and healing. Even if the content is disturbing and violent, it is still a part of *you*. Your dreams work like an internal therapist, offering you a chance to get comfortable with yourself – all the aspects of yourself, including your shadow.

Nightmares are therefore your dreaming mind's way of focusing on a red flag area of your waking life that urgently and seriously needs your attention and healing. For whatever reason, the gentle dream messages sent in the past haven't reached you, so a nightmare takes over to make the point loud and clear. In other words, your nightmares are simply aspects of yourself that are repressed or damaged and in urgent need of resolution and healing. In nightmares you get a chance to meet the potential for negativity that is within you but which you may not be acknowledging fully in your waking life. This is so very powerful for your personal growth because being aware of the shadow within you and choosing not to act on it is where all learning, evolution and inner strength begins. The battle between positive and negative is depicted insightfully in the famous Cherokee story of the two battling wolves inside us all: the evil wolf and the good wolf. The wolf that wins is the one we decide to feed. In short, the waking choices we make define us.

STAY COOL

Knowing the healing potential of nightmares, you can ask your dreaming mind to wake you up in a dream with your shadow in it, so you can acknowledge it, forgive it and release it. The more you start to break down barriers, face fears and overcome limitations in your dreams, the more likely you are to do the same in your waking life.

And when you do meet monsters or other things in your dreams that are terrifying because they are so extreme – and couldn't possibility exist or happen in your waking life – your lucid dream training may well kick in and tell you this has to be a dream.

If you do become lucid in a lurid nightmare, apply exactly the same rules as for any other lucid dream. *Keep your cool.* Carry out reality checks to remind yourself that you are safe in your bed and this is only a dream. Once you know this isn't real, stay with it. Stay with your nightmare. Don't let it collapse. Tell those monsters that you know they are a part of you. Ask them questions. Why are they here? What do they want? How can you help them? Offer them the hand of friendship. You may well find that when you offer your inner monsters a chance to connect with you, they reveal their lack of substance. Like an illusion or a mirage, they transform into empty shells on a sandy beach.

REFLECTIONS

By taking an honest look at yourself through the mirror of your nightmares, even if you don't always like what you see reflected back, you can connect to deeper and deeper levels of yourself that you can't access in real life.

The takeaway here is that nightmares are a fast pass opportunity to understand yourself better, find healing and resolution and grow in self-compassion and wisdom. Using lucid dreaming techniques to understand the endlessly inventive ways your shadow is revealed to you reinforces how wonderfully deep and mysterious you are. When you have the perception to look for what is beneath the surface of things, you don't only wake up to the real purpose of your dreams, you start waking up to what is meaningful in your waking life too. And as you get more comfortable 'waking up' and challenging your 'demons', you intuitively begin to sense that others have their hidden shadows and silent battles to overcome too, and all of us are growing up and dreaming deeply together.

This newfound compassion for yourself and feeling of intimate connection with others is a true gift.

PTSD

The possibility of transforming nightmares into healing experiences is one of the reasons scientists are now actively researching lucid dreaming techniques.[8] They believe lucid dreaming could be a viable treatment for nightmares associated with PTSD. Sufferers of PTSD are taught by therapists how to change the narrative of a nightmare while they are actually experiencing it in a lucid dream. They are also taught how to change the nightmare when they are awake by visualizing it and rewriting the ending positively in their daydreams.

Changing nightmares through lucid dreaming by night and visualization by day is a technique that can be very helpful for resolving and releasing recurring frightening dreams that are interfering with quality sleep. However, if you are suffering from PTSD or dangerously high stress levels, it is important to only do this with the support of a qualified therapist in case visualization causes flashbacks.

Note: There is a distinct difference between nightmares and night terrors. Nightmares tend to occur during REM sleep, whereas night terrors occur during non-REM sleep and involve screaming and physical movements. Should you experience night terrors, or any stress-related or genetic sleep disorder, please consult your doctor before practising lucid dreaming techniques.

Your Dream Works: *Shadow Facts*

WHAT YOU'VE LEARNED: Lucid dreaming gives you a safe opportunity to meet, understand, heal and resolve aspects of your personality that are limiting your personal growth.

TAKE NOTE: Write down or record what techniques help you scare off, overcome, or come to terms with your inner demons. Have you been able to transform monsters into miracles and a nightmare into nirvana?

#21

Your Time to Fly

The transformative power of lucid dreaming is absolutely incredible. You have such vast potential for growth, and lucid dreaming connects you directly to that untapped creativity. Like a baby growing in a womb, or a frog who lives in a well, you suddenly realize that there is actually a whole new world, an ocean out there you never knew existed before. It's time for you to take a leap of faith and explore the unknown. The possibilities are limitless.

So, now that you can see the potential behind all your dreams clearly and with self-awareness, today's practice will offer some suggestions of what you might choose to do in a lucid dream, or which aspect of yourself you might choose to meet. Then, the next time you find yourself awake in your dreams, you can simply imagine or think about that aspect of yourself and watch it appear.

Whatever happens next depends on you, but there's one thing you can be certain of: revelations will unfold.

YOUR INNER CHILD

Your inner child is the part of you that is forever young, vulnerable, trusting, spontaneous and passionate. Like your shadow side, it is within you whatever age you are, and constantly wanting validation.

You'll meet your inner child in dreams that feature childhood themes such as school and exams, as well as any symbol that looks neglected, abandoned, forgotten, lost and in need of unconditional love.

Not all of us got that unconditional love from parents and carers when we were growing up, and the lesson learned from this experience is that our needs don't matter. If this applies to you, you may bury your needs in work, in other people or in addictions. Your dreams offer you an opportunity to reconnect with your inner child, understand what they are trying to tell you, acknowledge their pain and parent yourself.

And if you become lucid in a dream, you can ask your inner child to trust you and reveal themselves to you. You'll know when you are meeting them, in whatever form, because your instinct will be to nurture, protect and guide. You can be there for them. You can acknowledge their vulnerability and protect them. You can even ask to meet yourself as a child and give yourself the chance to grow up again, but this time believing in yourself without needing external things or other people to validate you.

Meeting your inner child feels incredibly poignant. You can grow up with them. You can guide them. You can go on adventures with them. You can hug and reassure them. And if you meet animals in your dreams, know that they are symbols of pure emotion and instinct that need nurturing, understanding and resolution from you too.

In addition to meeting your inner child, you can meet past versions of yourself. You can be there for yourself and heal past wounds. Time, remember, doesn't exist in a dream. Past, present and future happen at the same time. This isn't science fiction. Some physicists believe that time is not linear, but a loop – but that's another book!

YOUR HIGHER SELF

Your higher self is the wise part of you or the part that knows what is in your best interests. In many ways, it oversees every one of your dreams in that it offers you a chance to get a fresh perspective on your life. However, in a lucid dream you can actually ask to meet your higher self and have a conversation with it so you can drink in the wisdom it has to share with you. More often than not, when you meet your higher self, it will have your voice or look like you or be a highly evolved version of yourself. You may even get to meet a future version of yourself. How does this feel? Incredible, but strangely familiar too.

YOUR CONFIDENT SELF

You can programme your dreams to grant your every desire, to manifest sexual partners, to meet anyone, do anything. Experimenting with infinite possibility can be thrilling, but don't go overboard, as everything you do in your dream, you are actually doing with yourself. And because your dreams are all about you, it might just be possible for you to use them not only to become more assertive and confident – because you have practised a scenario you feel uncertain about successfully in your dreams beforehand – but also to practise certain skills, situations or conversations. For example, you can practise telling someone you like them or handing in your resignation or standing up for yourself if you feel unfairly treated. Then in waking life you have the confidence of knowing you've rehearsed this. You've been here before.

The scientific evidence for this is still developing, but there are indications that practising skills without fear of injury or humiliation in a dream can improve performance, particularly in sports and music-making.[9] It seems that training in a lucid dream creates neuropathways in your brain that cross over into real life. Your lucid dreaming brain doesn't know the difference between a dream and waking life. So, the theory is you can learn something in a dream and your brain thinks you have really done it.

For decades sports psychologists have encouraged athletes to visualize winning and to mentally practise motor skills, but it seems that lucid dream training achieves far better results than waking imagination.[10] When you perform motor skills while dreaming, your brain's sensorimotor cortex, which controls movement, activates. This could be beneficial for people with physical disabilities. And if you can practise a sporting or motor skill in a dream and become a more accomplished athlete as a result, the sky really is the limit. You can practise literally anything, from learning a musical instrument, to becoming a successful novelist or director, to learning a new language, to calling upon feelings of calm when you panic, to becoming a kinder person. Whatever you want to do, start in real life first and then let the training and the mind games continue in your dreams.

YOUR CREATIVE SELF

Whenever you become lucid in a dream, another positive side-effect is enhanced creativity.[11] Many people, myself included, use lucid dreaming to ignite their imagination, and those who are more creative are more likely to lucid dream or be fascinated by their dreams. There is a reason for this two-way street. Clear dream recall, dream-decoding skills and the ability to daydream are all strong indicators that you are more likely to lucid dream.

Waking up in your dreams is the ultimate creativity high, because your dreams are fuelled by the part of your brain related to imagination, intuition and creativity. If you become aware you are dreaming, you bring your rational consciousness into all this unpredictable creative brain activity. And when you are in that enlightened place, you have an opportunity to unleash the full force of your creativity. You can ask your dream to bring you the inspiration you need. You can ask your dreaming mind what is the meaning of your life. You can ask it to create, or brainstorm, literally anything for you. All you are required to do is trust in your lucid dream and the inspiration it brings to you.

Wherever you are on your lucid dream journey, enjoy the thrill of discovery. Experiment to find out which technique or combination of techniques works best for you. Keep shaking things up. Let nothing ever be set in stone. And as you continue your inside-out experiment, never forget that lucid dreaming is a proven self-development tool and confidence-booster that is not only free, but always there for you.

SOARING

And as well as meeting and healing aspects of yourself and unleashing your creativity in a lucid dream, you can also be or do anything you want. What you decide to be or do is up to you, but I hope it will include lucid flying. You may have already had a dream in which you were flying without wings. It's a common dream and you probably woke up in the morning feeling terrific. And for good reason – flying dreams are good news for your brain, because they are often accompanied by positive emotions and can therefore help your brain process information better.

Whenever I have a flying dream, I am literally walking on air. A few years ago, my dream recall of flying felt so real that I went for a walk in a field that same morning and started to run in the belief I really could fly. Of course, in real life it didn't happen. But ever since then I have used flying as my reality check. If I tell myself I can fly and I can actually fly, I know I am in a lucid dream.

If you too want to learn to fly in your dreams, here are some guidelines to help you grow your own wings:

- Along with your regular lucid dream training, during the day and before you go to sleep, incubate a lucid dream. Tell yourself you are going to fly in your dreams tonight and when you do, you will know you are dreaming. You may want to take things one step further and plan or draw your dream and how, when and where you are going to fly. Or you can let your dreaming mind entertain you with the details.

- Then, when you find yourself in a dream, tell yourself that you can fly. Take a deep breath and believe it. If you are dreaming you *will* fly.

- Let your dream take you to see whatever bigger picture of your life you need to see. As you fly high above yourself, know that you have been here before. Remind yourself that you are remembering what comes naturally to you.

- This is also a great time to ask your dream questions and to listen keenly to the answers. You can talk to yourself in the dream, too, and tell yourself that you are infinitely creative and that your life is happy and fulfilling.

- Drink in every detail of your lucid flying dream.
- When you wake up the next day, carry that euphoria with you into real life. *You can rule your world.*

In your Dreams

You might just want to keep this book by your bedside or stored on your phone so you can refer to it whenever you need a gentle reminder that you are an adventurer born with a dreamer's soul. You can also use it as a dream recall trigger or even a reality check. Every time you pick it up or read it, ask yourself, 'Is this a dream?'

ONE LAST VISION FOR YOU TO TAKE AWAY

'When I'm old and dying, I plan to look back on my life and say, "Wow, that was an adventure," not, "Wow, I sure felt safe."'

Tom Preston-Werner

When Steve Jobs passed away, his sister revealed that he departed with a lingering look and the simple, mysterious observation, 'Oh, wow!' Was he dreaming with his eyes open? It is often said by people in their senior years that the older you get, the more dream-like waking life feels.

From now on, no more playing it safe. It's your time for adventure. Whether your eyes are wide open or wide shut, may your first – as well as your last – impulse always be, 'Oh, wow! Oh, wow! Oh, wow!'

Your Dream Works: *Your Time to Fly*

WHAT YOU'VE LEARNED: You can explore infinite possibilities within a lucid dream and carry whatever wisdom, healing, skills or sense of mystery you have learned, discovered and experienced over into your waking life.

TAKE NOTE: Make a note of what you would like to encounter, unlock, experience or learn in your next lucid dream. Prove to yourself that lucid dreaming it first means you *can* do it and make your waking life bigger and better.

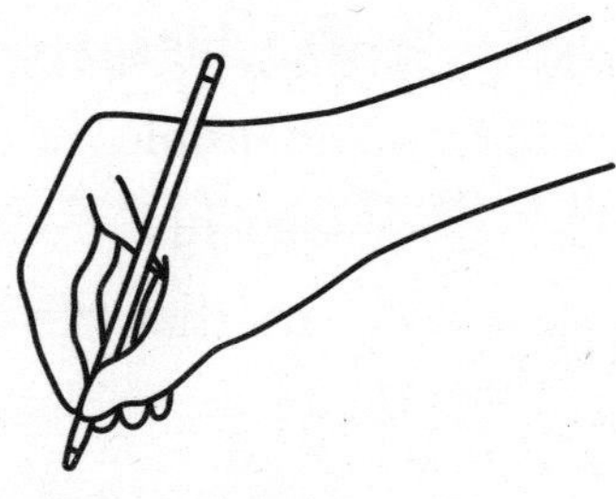

YOUR WEEK THREE DREAMER'S CHECKPOINT

Oh, wow! You are awesome. Reaching this point in the book is a massive achievement. I salute you! Be sure to seriously congratulate yourself. Under no circumstances should you ever underestimate the value of reaching this third and final checkpoint, whether you have experimented with the full-blown lucid dreaming techniques or simply digested them for future use. Whether you realize it or not, you are giving your dreaming mind the essential nutrients it needs to help your dreams grow into life-changing experiences.

As with the previous two weeks, check off what you have digested and experienced to help you keep track. Then press ahead with the afterword and start the three weeks again, or use what you have learned to devise your own bigger and better dreaming plan. Just make sure, as you move forward that you don't ever let your dreams and your love of dreaming die.

#15: DECODING TIME

- O Revisit your Dreams
- O Dream-Decoding Fundamentals
- O Dream Themes
- O Association

#16: INCEPTION

- O The MILD Technique
- O The Wake Up, Back to Bed Technique
- O Play the FILD

#17: GO WILD

- O Night Owl
- O Counting in your Sleep
- O Cycling in your Sleep

#18: THRESHOLDS

- O Sleep Paralysis
- O Meet the 'H' Team

#19: DON'T LET YOUR DREAM GO

You're lucid – learn how to stay in your dream.

#20: SHADOW FACTS

Make friends with your shadow side and transform your nightmares into lucid dreams.

#21: YOUR TIME TO FLY

Use lucid dreaming to heal your life, enhance your creativity, improve skills and grow your own wings.

Dreams Never Lie

Sometimes in a movie or a TV show, a character's dream is portrayed as so real that the audience is as surprised as the character when they wake up. The dream sequence adds psychological depth and reveals to the audience what is clearly true, but hidden deeply in the character's heart and soul.

There is a remarkable and refreshing honesty and heartfelt logic about dreams. In them, you get to see your hopes and your fears, and yourself as you are. It takes real courage to enter your dream world. I applaud every one of you for reaching this point in the book. Sometimes when you dream, the honesty is so intense and illuminating that your only option is to radically change your life for the better. And if you can become lucid in your dreams, you can transform every dream you have, lucid or not, into a positive and healing experience. There really are no downsides to dream work. But perhaps the biggest bonus of all is that you acquire a loving companion for life.

Don't we all want someone who is always there for us? Someone who considers our every need and understands everything about us? Don't we all want a loyal friend who isn't afraid to tell us the truth, even if we don't want to hear it? Your dreams are that loyal companion – a best friend who will inspire and guide you and never tell you anything but the absolute truth. And in today's world, where spin and fake news often overtake truth, and appearance frequently eclipses substance, you need your trustworthy dream companion more than ever.

Your dreams can't lie. Paradoxically, they always keep things real! And, like the true friend they are, they believe in you and want you to believe in yourself.

BELIEVE IN YOURSELF

If you have already had flashes of lucidity, or over time the techniques you have learned in this book take you there, you'll know it's a pretty intense feeling. Whenever you experience it, the chances are you're going to want to return to that feeling time and again. That's understandable. Even though decoding the messages from your non-lucid dreams has tremendous value for your evolution, once you've actually 'woken up' in a dream, you're unlikely to want to return to non-lucid dreaming. You've tasted success. You know you can do it. You can become conscious in a dream. You can become lucid.

And with that stunning realization you know that it is now entirely possible for you to successfully navigate the vast and infinite and timeless oceans of your mind. As you set sail, you know you can face your fears and insecurities, solve problems, make creative connections and practise skills that cross over into real life. You know you can transform your nightmares and relieve anxieties. You know you can meet departed loved ones or any person you have ever wanted to talk to. You can have tremendous fun, too – you can become a singing flower or a flying lion. You can roam freely anywhere you want, do anything or be anyone. You truly are in your own mysterious virtual reality, where nothing is ever out of bounds. It's spectacular. It's transformative. With your creativity fully unleashed, you feel unstoppable.

WEIGHING YOU DOWN

Yet more often than not, something unavoidable intervenes. No, it's not dream collapse this time. It's something more disappointing and damaging than that. It's something ugly that unexpectedly rears its head and blocks you from waking up and living your dreams just when you feel so close to touching them.

It's self-doubt!

If you have even the slightest lingering doubt that waking up in your dreams is possible for you, or if you still can't quite believe your dreams make sense or are of true value, then that doubt will clip your dreaming wings.

Self-belief is the evolutionary journey of us all, so please don't get frustrated with yourself if you still suffer doubt from time to time. It's normal. Step into that observer role instead, and don't identify with the doubts. Understand that if you don't trust yourself, you make it harder for your dreams to come alive for you.

Self-belief comes easier to some than others. It can be comforting to know that if you struggle with it, perhaps because of past traumas or negative messages from parents, carers or teachers, your dreaming mind will never walk away or give up on you. Whether you recall your dreams or not, it will still be working away every night to help you heal those inner dramas and hurts.

Remember, your dreams want you to fall in love with yourself and your infinite potential. They want you to dissolve energy-draining doubts and fears. They want you to lose the albatrosses around your neck that weigh you down. They want you to believe in yourself completely and choose to fly before you walk in all your lucid dreams.

SOUL-SEARCHING

Always treat any dream revelations shared with you by other people with deep respect. They may not realize it, but they are sharing a part of their soul. It feels good, doesn't it, when someone tells you that they have dreamed about you. Of course, they aren't dreaming about you as such, but of something about you – something you have said or done or what you represent or symbolize to them has spoken to them on a deep soul level.

And while on the subject of soul-searching, I'd like to close this book by discussing the small percentage of dreams – around 1 per cent – that are *supernormal*. The remaining 99 per cent of dreams are symbolic and psychological, and they have rightly been the focus of this book, but supernormal dreams are ones that appear to cross the boundaries between space and time, life and death. Telepathic, precognitive, shared and afterlife dreams fall into this category. They are far more common than most of the literature and research on dreaming is willing to admit.

Over the decades I've been a dream author, I've not only collated a huge database of symbolic dreams, but also a file of thousands of supernormal dreams that seem to defy explanation, sent to me by readers. In telepathic dreams, the dreamer discovers things that they couldn't possibly know. In precognitive dreams, the future plays out accurately. In shared dreams, two or more people seem to experience the same dream at the same time. In afterlife dreams or parting visions, the dreamer meets a departed loved one and the meeting is so vivid and realistic it feels like proof of the afterlife. And then there are dreams of past lives and unborn children, and so-called 'worker' dreams in which the dreamer offers spiritual healing to those in need.

There is ongoing research into these kinds of dreams and I've been at the forefront of some of it, particularly afterlife and precognitive dreams.[1] These dreams are outside the scope of this book, but they certainly add substance to the idea that perhaps, just perhaps, there is a part of us that is infinite and eternal and that can connect us to everyone and everything and cross the boundaries of space, time, life and death.

If you do have a psychic dream, it's likely it will feel very different from a symbolic or lucid dream. It will typically feel realistic and have a beginning, middle and end, whereas symbolic dreams are often more like fragments or music videos. As with lucid dreaming, if you think you have had a supernormal or spiritual dream, keep your cool. Write it down. Ponder its meaning and celebrate it. We are still very much in the learning stages when it comes to dreaming, so your best bet is to trust your initial instinct. If your dream felt transcendent, accept it as the precious spiritual gift it was.

Two Tribes

There is a Brazilian tribe called the Piraha,[2] who have been described as the happiest people on Earth. They don't sleep for long periods, because they believe that every night's sleep is a death. In the morning, they wake up to find the 'old' them – yesterday's version – has died and they have been reborn. If they do sleep for longer periods, they give themselves a new name and refer to their old name in the past tense.

I'm certainly not recommending that you ditch a good night's sleep like the Piraha, as sleep is essential for dreaming. But I do want to draw your attention to their thinking about sleep. It could be said that when you sleep and cross over to your dream world, you 'die' another day. Every time you go to bed, you are regenerating. Your body and brain don't rest. They are busy renewing and repairing. It's up to you whether you wake from your dreams a more evolved and aware person than you were the day before. But you can be born anew physically, emotionally and mentally in the morning. What an awesome thought.

I'd also like to mention the Malaysian Senoi.[3] This tribe places lucid dreaming centre stage in their lives. Children as young as four are encouraged to narrate their dreams every morning to the elders of the tribe and to re-enter their dreams the following night to face any fears. What is remarkable about the Senoi is the low to non-existent incidence of both crime and depression. Could the value they place on the healing and transformative potential of lucid dreaming be the reason?

YOUR END IS YOUR BEGINNING

In my humble opinion, dreams don't happen to you, they are created by and for you. They can change your mind, fire your creativity and inspire your life. They are *your* dreams. It's *your* life. *You* decide. Most of us are afraid to know the truth of our infinite potential, afraid to shine. Afraid to live fully and dream deeply. If this resonates, the biggest roadblock to your own fulfilment is *you*. But your dreams offer you a chance to truly get over yourself every single night.

Whether dreams are psychological projections created by your brain[4] and/or psychic experiences opening your eyes to a transcendent spiritual realm where you are interconnected with everyone and everything, they are an incredible opportunity for you to unlock the secrets of your heart and discover just how fascinating you really are. You need never be bored again once you start noticing the beauty and potential of your own dreams.

In this social-media-obsessed age, many of us want to be seen and heard. In your dreams you can see and validate yourself every single night. To reference the poetry of T. S. Eliot, dream work is a journey to the centre of yourself where after all that 'ceaseless exploration' you discover who you truly are for the first time.

Remember my pledge at the beginning of this book? How I am on a mission to get the world to fall in love with their dreams and, by extension, themselves? I hope I have started and ended in the same place and what you have discovered on your journey here has helped you fall head over heels in love with the vast untapped potential of your own night vision.

YOUR NEVER-ENDING STORY

Lucid dreaming can help you achieve a sense of deep peace and well-being. It can also make your waking life feel like an adventure and your sleeping life pure bliss. The more you are aware of and actively participate in your dreams, the more you can wake up in them, and the greater their transformative impact on your waking life will be.

Connecting to your dreams really is just the start of an incredible journey within. And I know your journey won't stop here. Keep dreaming, keep exploring. The resources that follow offer a few more insights, and details of how to get in touch with me if you have any questions or dream stories to share. I'm not saying goodbye, because perhaps we'll meet again in our waking life or in our dreams.

'All that we see or seem
Is but a dream within a dream.'

Edgar Allan Poe

Notes and References

Introduction

1. M. Neider, E. F. Pace-Schott, E. Forselius, B. Pittman and P. T. Morgan, 'Lucid Dreaming and Ventromedial versus Dorsolateral Prefrontal Task Performance', *Consciousness and Cognition*, 20: 2 (2011), 234–44; published online 9 Sept., 2010; https://www.ncbi.nlm.nih.gov/pmc/articles/PMC3026881/.
2. U. Voss, R. Holzmann, I. Tuin and A. J. Hobson, 'Lucid Dreaming: A state of consciousness with features of both waking and non-lucid dreaming', *Sleep*, 32: 9 (1 Sept., 2009), 1,191–200; https://www.ncbi.nlm.nih.gov/pmc/articles/PMC2737577/.
3. Ibid.
4. B. Baird *et al.*, 'Frequent Lucid Dreaming associated with Increased Functional Connectivity between Frontopolar Cortex and Temporoparietal Association Areas', *Scientific Reports*, 8 (2018), 77–98.
5. P. Bourke and H. Shaw, 'Spontaneous Lucid Dreaming Frequency and Waking Insight', *Dreaming*, 24: 2 (2014), 152–9.
6. J. Mutz *et al.*, 'Exploring the Neural Correlates of Dream Phenomenology and Altered States of Consciousness during Sleep', *Neuroscience of Consciousness*, 1 (2017), nix009b.
7. D. Martin *et al.*, 'Cognitive and Emotional Processes during Dreaming: A neuroimaging view', *Consciousness and Cognition*, 20: 4 (2011), 998–1,008; https://pubmed.ncbi.nlm.nih.gov/21075010/.

Week One

1. Fabian Guénolé *et al.*, 'Dreams in Normal and Pathological Aging', *Psychol. Neuropsychiatr. Vieil.*, 8: 2 (2010), 87–96.
2. J. Gackenbach *et al.*, 'Video Game Play Effects on Dreams: Self-evaluation and content analysis', *Eludamos: Journal for Computer Game Culture*, 2: 2 (2008), 169–86; 'Video Game Play and Lucid Dreams: Implications for the development of consciousness', *Dreaming*, 16: 2 (2006), 96–110; M. Sestir *et al.*, 'Relationship between Video Game Play Factors and Frequency of Lucid and Control Dreaming Experiences', *Dreaming*, 29: 2 (2019), 127–43; M. Tai *et al.*, 'The Relationship between Video Game Use, Game Genre, and Lucid/Control Dreaming', *Sleep*, 40: 1 (28 April, 2017), A271; https://www.livescience.com/6521-video-gamers-control-dreams-study-suggests.html.
3. Sestir, ibid.
4. R. Stickgold *et al.*, 'Replaying the Game: Hypnagogic images in normals and amnesics', *Science*, 290 (13 Oct., 2000), 350–53.
5. https://news.xbox.com/en-us/2020/12/07/powering-the-dreams-of-gamers-with-xbox/.
6. In 2021 the legendary French designer and perfume maker Serge Lutens created an exclusive new fragrance called *La proie pour l'ombre* (Prey for the Shadows), which was inspired by a visionary dream he'd had about two exotic women. As far as I know, it is the first perfume based on a dream. Forgive the pun, but it was a dream come true when I was contacted by the Serge Lutens company prior to launch to offer their marketing and international sales team my insight about the magical power of dreams in our lives. (Not to mention as a dream author, I now have my very own 'because you dream it' perfume.)
7. David Z. Hambrick, 'Brain Training Doesn't Make You Smarter', *Scientific American* (2 Dec., 2014); https://www.scientificamerican.com/article/brain-training-doesn-t-make-you-smarter/.
8. T. Blankert *et al.*, 'Imagining Success: Multiple achievement goals and the effectiveness of imagery', *Basic Appl. Soc. Psych.*, 39: 1 (2 Jan., 2017), 60–67.

9. S. Brand *et al.*, 'Dream Recall and its Relationship to Sleep, Perceived Stress and Creativity among Adolescents', *Journal of Adolescent Health*, 49: 5 (Nov. 2011), 525–31.
10. https://aphantasia.com/.
11. US National Library of Medicine, 'The Possible Functions of REM Sleep and Dreaming'; https://www.ncbi.nlm.nih.gov/books/NBK11121/.
12. William H. McRaven, *Make Your Bed* (Michael Joseph, 2017).
13. B. Smith *et al.*, 'Lucid Dream Frequency and Alarm Clock Snooze Button Use', *Dreaming*, 25: 4 (2015), 291–9.
14. Denholm J. Aspy *et al.*, 'Effects of Vitamin B6 (Pyridoxine) and a B Complex Preparation on Dreaming and Sleep', *Perceptual and Motor Skills*, 125: 3 (2018), 451–62.
15. T. Nakano *et al.*, 'Blink-related Momentary Activation of the Default Mode Network while Viewing Videos', *Proceedings of the National Academy of Sciences*, 110: 2 (8 Jan., 2013), 702–6.
16. C. Cascio *et al.*, 'Self-affirmation Activates Brain Systems associated with Self-related Processing and Reward and is Reinforced by Future Orientation', *Social Cognitive and Affective Neuroscience*, 11: 4 (2016), 621–9.

Week Two

1. C. Morewedge *et al.*, 'When Dreaming is Believing: The (motivated) interpretation of dreams', *Journal of Personality and Social Psychology*, 96: 2 (2009), 249–64.
2. J. Mossbridge *et al.*, 'Predictive Physiological Anticipation Preceding Seemingly Unpredictable Stimuli: A meta-analysis', *Frontiers in Psychology*, *3: 390* (2012).
3. A. Dijksterhuis *et al.*, 'On Making the Right Choice, Deliberation without Attention Effect', *Science*, 31 (Feb. 2017).
4. To quote the office of Naval Research, 'Research in human pattern recognition and decision making suggest that there is a sixth sense

through which humans can detect and act on unique patterns without consciously and intentionally analysing them.'

5. https://journals.ub.uni-heidelberg.de/index.php/IJoDR/article/view/10151.
6. Z. Zhang *et al.*, 'Longitudinal Effects of Meditation on Brain Resting State Functional Connectivity', *International Journal of Scientific Reports*, 11, 11361 (2021).
7. https://www.health.harvard.edu/staying-healthy/what-meditation-can-do-for-your-mind-mood-and-health.
8. R. Colbert *et al.*, 'Effect of the Transcendental Meditation Program on Graduation, College Acceptance and Dropout Rates for Students Attending an Urban Public High School', *Education*, 133: 4 (Summer 2013), 495–501.
9. https://www.bbc.co.uk/news/world-us-canada-12661646.
10. https://www.medicalnewstoday.com/articles/321388.
11. B. Sundram *et al.*, 'Effectiveness of Progressive Muscle Relaxation Therapy as a Worksite Health Promotion Program', *Ind. Health*, 54: 3 (16 May, 2016), 204–14.
12. https://www.frontiersin.org/articles/10.3389/fpsyt.2017.00159/full.
13. https://www.ncbi.nlm.nih.gov/pmc/articles/PMC6134749/.
14. https://www.frontiersin.org/articles/10.3389/fpsyt.2017.00159/full.
15. Ursula Voss *et al.*, 'Measuring Consciousness in Dreams: The lucidity and consciousness in dreams scale', *Consciousness and Cognition*, 1 (22 Mar., 2013), 8–21.
16. https://www.cam.ac.uk/cammagazine/benefitsofboredom.
17. Kalina Christoff *et al.*, 'Experience Sampling during fMRI Reveals Default Network and Executive System Contributions to Mind Wandering', *Proceedings of the National Academy of Sciences* , 106: 21 (2009), 8719–24.
18. C. Godwin *et al.*, 'Functional Connectivity within and between Intrinsic Brain Networks Correlates with Trait Mind Wandering', *Neuropsycholigia*, 103 (August 2017), 140–53.
19. J. Jenkins, 'The Mozart Effect', *Journal of the Royal Society of Medicine*, 94: 4 (April 2001), 170–72.

20. B. Cahn, B. Rael and John Polich, 'Meditation States and Traits: EEG, ERP and neuroimaging studies', *Psychological Bulletin*, 132: 2 (2006), 180–211; J. Lagopoulos, J. Xu, I. Rasmussen, A. Vik, G. S. Malhi, C. F. Eliassen, I. E. Arntsen, J. G. Saether, S. Hollup, A. Holen, S. Davanger and Ø. Ellingsen, 'Increased Theta and Alpha EEG Activity during Nondirective Meditation', *Journal of Alternative and Complementary Medicine*, 15: 11 (2009), 1,187–92; James Lane, Stefan Kasian, Justine Owens and Gail Marsh, 'Binaural Auditory Beats affect Vigilance, Performance and Mood', *Physiology and Behavior*, 63: 2 (1998), 249–52.
21. C. Kanduri *et al.*, 'The Effect of Listening to Music on Human Transcriptome', *PeerJ*, 12: 3 (March 2015).
22. British Psychological Society, 'Musical Training Can Increase Blood Flow to the Brain', *Science Daily* (8 May, 2014; www.sciencedaily.com/releases/2014/05/140507211622.htm; D. Gerry *et al.*, 'Active Music Classes in Infancy Enhance Musical, Communicative and Social Development', *Developmental Science*, 15: 3 (May 2012), 348–407.
23. D. Asby *et al.*, 'Is Dream Recall Underestimated by Retrospective Measures and Enhanced by Keeping a Logbook? An empirical investigation', *Consciousness and Cognition*, 42 (May 2016), 181–203.

Week Three

1. https://dreams.ucsc.edu/Library/domhoff_2001a.html.
2. T. Stumbrys *et al.*, 'Induction of Lucid Dreams: A systematic review of evidence', *Consciousness and Cognition*, 21: 3 (September 2012), 1,456–75; D. Aspy *et al.*, 'Reality Testing and the Mnemonic Induction of Lucid Dreams: Findings from the national Australian lucid dream induction study', *Dreaming*, 27: 3 (September 2017), 206–31.
3. https://journals.plos.org/plosone/article?id=10.1371/journal.pone.0201246.
4. https://www.asdreams.org/journal/articles/barrett3-2.htm.
5. S. A. Mota-Rolim *et al.*, 'Portable Devices to Induce Lucid Dreams—Are They Reliable?', *Frontiers in Neuroscience* (8 May, 2019).

6. D. Erlacher and T. Stumbrys, 'Wake Up, Work on Dreams, Back to Bed and Lucid Dream: A sleep laboratory study', *Frontiers in Psychology*, 11 (2020); D. Aspy, 'Findings from the International Lucid Dream Induction Study', *Frontiers in Psychology*, 11 (2020).
7. D. Denis *et al.*, 'Terror and Bliss? Commonalities and distinctions between sleep paralysis, lucid dreaming, and their associations with waking life experiences', *Journal of Sleep Research*, 26: 1 (Feb. 2017), 38–47; published online 27 July, 2016.
8. T. De Macedo *et al.*, 'My Dream, My Rules: Can lucid dreaming treat nightmares?', *Frontiers in Psychology*, 10 (26 Nov., 2019).
9. T. Stumbrys *et al.*, 'Effectiveness of Motor Practice in Lucid Dreams: A comparison with physical and mental practice', *Journal of Sports Science*, 34: 1 (2016), 27–34.
10. https://pubmed.ncbi.nlm.nih.gov/25846062/.
11. Paul and Charla Devereux, *Lucid Dreaming: Accessing your inner virtual realities* (Daily Grail Publishing, 2011).

Afterword

1. Theresa Cheung and Julia Mossbridge, *The Premonition Code* (Watkins, 2017).
2. Daniel Everett, *Don't Sleep, There Are Snakes: Life and language in the Amazonian jungle* (Profile, 2009).
3. https://www.world-of-lucid-dreaming.com/how-remote-senoi-tribes-use-dreams-for-personal-growth.html.
4. https://www.bbc.co.uk/news/science-environment-22031074.

Resources

DREAM ON: HOW TO CONTACT THE AUTHOR

If you have a dream question, story or insight, please don't hesitate to get in touch with me.

You can contact me via catchyourdream710@gmail.com. You can also message me via my website, www.theresacheung.com, or my author pages on Facebook and Instagram @thetheresacheung. I aim to reply to everyone in due course.

Don't feel that any dream you have is trivial, or that any question you want to ask about your night vision isn't important. I welcome and value discussing all your dreams, both those that are lucid and those that are not.

YOUR FREE 'DREAM NOTES'

If you send an email to catchyourdream710@gmail.com with the heading 'Dream Notes', I will send you a free half-hour audio recording of dream-inducing classical piano music that you can listen to every night before you go to sleep. This blissful lullaby is a free gift exclusive to readers and listeners of this book and is performed by my son, Royal College of Music graduate piano scholar Robert Cheung.

You may also want to subscribe to my free newsletter for updates, free gifts and more via my website, www.theresacheung.com.

You can also listen to all the episodes of my *White Shores* podcast, many of which feature dream-related themes, at this link: www.buzzsprout.com/361061. If you don't want to log into Buzzsprout, *White Shores* is also available on all podcast platforms. It features interviews with some of the world's leading scientists researching dreams and the supernormal, as well as experts and practitioners, music, laughter and more.

You may also wish to listen to the *Celebrity in Your Dreamzz* podcast hosted by Sky presenter Alex Morgan, which features my dream-decoding insights.

BIBLIOGRAPHY

These are arguably the key lucid dreaming research studies, but do bear in mind that lucid dream research is still in its infancy. There really is no telling what scientists will discover about its exciting potential in years and endless dreams to come.

D. Aspy, 'Findings from the International Lucid Dream Induction Study', *Frontiers in Psychology*, 11 (2020); https://www.ncbi.nlm.nih.gov/pmc/articles/PMC7379166/.

B. Baird, S. A. Mota-Rolim and M. Dresler, 'The Cognitive Neuroscience of Lucid Dreaming', *Neurosci. Biobehav. Rev.*, 100 (2019), 305–23; doi: 10.1016/j.neubiorev.2019.03.008.

D. Erlacher and T. Stumbrys, 'Wake Up, Work on Dreams, Back to Bed and Lucid Dream: A sleep laboratory study', *Frontiers in Psychology*, 11 (2020).

J. A. Hobson, E. F. Pace-Schott and R. Stickgold, 'Dreaming and the Brain: Toward a cognitive neuroscience of conscious states', *Behav. Brain Sci.*, 23 (2000), 793–842.

S. LaBerge, B. Baird and P. G. Zimbardo, 'Smooth Tracking of Visual Targets Distinguishes Lucid REM Sleep Dreaming and Waking Perception from Imagination', *Nat. Commun.*, 9: 3298 (2018); doi: 10.1038/s41467-018-05547-0.

S. LaBerge, K. LaMarca and B. Baird, 'Pre-sleep Treatment with Galantamine Stimulates Lucid Dreaming: A double-blind, placebo-controlled, crossover study', *PLoS ONE*, 13: e0201246 (2019); doi: 10.1371/journal.pone.0201246.

S. A. Mota-Rolim and J. F. Araujo, 'Neurobiology and Clinical Implications of Lucid Dreaming', *Med. Hypotheses*, 81 (2013), 751–6; doi: 10.1016/j.mehy.2013.04.049.

S. A. Mota-Rolim, A. Pavlou, G. Nascimento, J. Fontenele-Araujo and S. Ribeiro, 'Portable Devices to Induce Lucid Dreams—Are They Reliable?', *Frontiers in Neuroscience* (8 May 2019); https://www.ncbi.nlm.nih.gov/pmc/articles/PMC6517539/.

S. A. Mota-Rolim, Z. H. Targino, B. C. Souza, W. Blanco, J. F. Araujo and S. Ribeiro, 'Dream Characteristics in a Brazilian Sample: An online survey focusing on lucid dreaming', *Frontiers in Human Neuroscience*, 7: 836 (2013); doi: 10.3389/fnhum.2013.00836.

F. Paul, M. Schädlich and D. Erlacher, 'Lucid Dream Induction by Visual and Tactile Stimulation: An exploratory sleep laboratory study', *Int. J. Dream Res.*, 7 (2014), 61–6; doi: 10.11588/ijodr.2014.1.13044.

M. Rak, P. Beitinger, A. Steiger, M. Schredl and M. Dresler, 'Increased Lucid Dreaming Frequency in Narcolepsy', *Sleep*, 38: 5 (2015), 787–92; https://www.ncbi.nlm.nih.gov/pmc/articles/PMC4402667/.

N. Soffer-Dudek, 'Are Lucid Dreams Good for Us? Are We Asking the Right Question? A call for caution in lucid dream research', *Frontiers in Neuroscience* (2020); https://www.ncbi.nlm.nih.gov/pmc/articles/PMC6993576/.

G. Sparrow, R. Hurd, R. Carlson and A. Molina, 'Exploring the Effects of Galantamine Paired with Meditation and Dream Reliving on Recalled Dreams: Toward an integrated protocol for lucid dream induction and nightmare resolution', *Consciousness and Cognition*, 63 (2018), 74–88; doi: 10.1016/j.concog.2018.05.012.

T. Stumbrys and D. Erlacher, 'Lucid Dreaming during NREM Sleep: Two case reports', *Int. J. Dream Res.* 5 (2012), 151–5; doi: 10.11588/ijodr.2012.2.9483.

T. Stumbrys, D. Erlacher, M. Schädlich and M. Schredl, 'Induction of Lucid Dreams: A systematic review of evidence', *Consciousness and Cognition*, 21 (2012), 1,456–75; doi: 10.1016/j.concog.2012.07.003.

M. Tai, D. F. Mastin and J. Peszka, 'The Relationship between Video Game Use, Game Genre, and Lucid/Control Dreaming', *Sleep*, 40: 1 (2017), A271; https://academic.oup.com/sleep/article/40/suppl_1/A271/3782160.

University of Adelaide, 'Want to Control Your Dreams? Here's how you can', *Science Daily*, 17 October, 2017; https://www.sciencedaily.com/releases/2017/10/171019100812.htm.

R. Vallat and P. M. Ruby, 'Is It a Good Idea to Cultivate Lucid Dreaming?', *Frontiers in Psychology* (2019); https://www.ncbi.nlm.nih.gov/pmc/articles/PMC6874013/.

DREAM READS

Here are some books about sleep and dreaming that have spoken to me. This list is personal and by no means definitive. It also includes one of mine! Think of it as a starting point. Never stop reading and learning about the riches and possibilities of your own dreaming mind.

Cheung, Theresa, *The Dream Dictionary from A to Z* (HarperCollins, 2019).

Freke, Tim, *Lucid Living* (Watkins, 2016).

Freud, Sigmund, *The Interpretation of Dreams* (1899; Penguin, 1991).

Johnson, Clare R., *The Art of Transforming Nightmares* (Llewellyn, 2021).

—, *The Complete Book of Lucid Dreams* (Llewellyn, 2017).

Krippner, Stanley F. *et al.*, *Extraordinary Dreams and How to Work with Them* (Sunnypress, 2002).

LaBerge, Stephen, *Exploring the World of Lucid Dreams* (Ballantine, 1994).

Leschziner, Guy, *The Nocturnal Brain* (Simon and Schuster, 2019).

Mavromatis, Andreas, *Hypnagogia: The unique state of consciousness between wakefulness and sleep* (Thyrsos Press, 2010).

Morley, Charlie, *Lucid Dreaming Made Easy* (Hay House, 2018).

Radin, Dean, *Real Magic: Ancient Wisdom, Modern Science* (Harmony, 2018).

Ross, Robert, *Dreaming the Soul Back Home: Shamanic dreaming for healing and becoming whole* (New World Library, 2002).

Targ, Russell, *Limitless Mind: A guide to remote viewing and transformation of consciousness* (New World Library, 2004).

Tuccilo, Dylan, *The Field Guide to Lucid Dreaming* (Workman, 2013).

Waggoner, Robert, *Lucid Dreaming* (Moment Press, 2008).

Wahbeh, Helane, *The Science of Channelling* (New Harbinger, 2021).

Walker, Matthew, *Why We Sleep* (Penguin, 2018).

DEEP DREAM EXPLORATION

If you want to delve deeper, here are some online organizations I recommend, as long as you remember to keep your dream vibe cool, don't lose yourself in the ideas of others and always trust your own innate creativity and dream knowing.

https://www.world-of-lucid-dreaming.com

This lucid dreaming online course, edited by entrepreneur, martial artist and visionary Chris Hammond, is one of the most popular and respected online. When you sign up you get a free ten-day introduction to the lucid dreaming course via email. After that, it isn't free anymore, but costs are minimal and you certainly get your money's worth in terms of advice, support, information and a community of enthusiastic dream lovers. Well worth checking out.

www.asdreams.org

The International Association for the Study of Dreams (IASD) is an amazing online dream community you may want to join for its brilliant advice and information, as well as its *DreamTime* magazine and academic publication, *Dreaming*. What I love the most about it is that it connects dreamers from all over the world and it also runs online conferences.

https://www.charliemorley.com

A popular and engaging lucid dreaming teacher and bestselling author who runs regular lucid dreaming courses and retreats both on and offline.

https://deepluciddreaming.com

A vibrant and highly creative online dream community hosted by lucid dreaming professor Dr Clare Johnson. I've interviewed her twice on my *White Shores* podcast and you couldn't ask for a more knowledgeable, creative and enchanting dream guide.

www.dreaminglucid.com

This online magazine community seeks to educate, inform and inspire lucid dreamers by constantly sharing techniques and lucid dream stories.

www.themysteryexperience.com

A theme throughout this book has been lucid living as well as dreaming, and philosopher Tim Freke, whom I've interviewed twice on my *White Shores* podcast, is the author of *Lucid Living*. He also runs international courses and retreats, as well as his 'What is life?' YouTube channel, which I've been a guest on.

Explore Lucid Dreaming YouTube channel

There's a vast amount of lucid dreaming material available for free on YouTube, so you need to be discerning, but this lucid dreaming channel is one you certainly won't regret subscribing to.

Acknowledgements

Deepest gratitude to my truly visionary editor, Kezia Bayard-White, for commissioning and editing this book with profound insight. I am also infinitely grateful to my exceedingly wise literary agent, Jane Graham Maw (www.grahammawchristie.com), for her support, wisdom and calm these last five years. Thank you also to the wonderful Amandeep Singh, Holly Blood, Lucy Brown and everyone at HarperCollins involved in the production and promotion of my Thorsons titles. I am also greatly indebted to PR expert Becke Parker, Helen Rochester for her support and to the talented Ingrid Court-Jones for her invaluable input while I was researching and writing this book.

How to Catch a Dream would not have been possible without my bestselling *Dream Dictionary from A to Z*, first published by HarperCollins in 2006, and the many readers it has inspired to message me over the years about their fascinating dreams and lucid dream experiences. I can't thank my dream readers enough. You are the stuff that real dreams are made of and a never-failing source of inspiration to me as an author.

Gratitude also to the scientists and dream experts out there tirelessly researching dreaming and states of consciousness, in particular Dr Julia Mossbridge, Dr Clare Johnson, Dr Dean Radin,

Dr Garret Yount and Dr Helane Wahbeh and her amazing IONS (Institute of Noetic Science) team. I'd also like to pay tribute to every single guest who has appeared on my podcast, *White Shores*. I am forever in debt to author and journalist Ella Dove for believing in my love of dreams. Big thank you to my son, Robert, for brilliantly producing *White Shores* and for bringing the joy of music into my life and the lives of my podcast listeners, and to creative spark Matthew Cooper for his creativity and social-media skills. Sincere gratitude also to Mona, Alyssa, Lindsey and Melody at Conscious Living PR for being a pure joy and waking dream to work with. Last, but by no means least, heartfelt thanks once more to my inspiring son Robert, and to my gorgeous daughter, Ruthie, for being an Earth angel, and to my husband, Ray (and my little dog, Arnie), for their constant support and love and for proving to me every single day that dreams really do come true.

About the Author

Theresa Cheung is a *Sunday Times* bestselling dream-decoding author. She has a degree from King's College, Cambridge, and is the author of numerous bestselling titles translated into 40 languages, including *The Dream Dictionary from A to Z* (HarperCollins, 2006), *The Dream Decoder Card Pack* (Laurence King Publishing, 2019) and *The Premonition Code* (Watkins, 2018).

Theresa works closely with scientists researching consciousness and dreaming and has contributed features about dreams to *Bustle*, *Vice*, *Cosmopolitan*, *Good Housekeeping*, *Red*, *Grazia*, *Heat*, *InStyle*, *Yahoo*, the *Daily Mail*, the *Daily Mirror*, *Glamour*, and many more. A popular guest on ITV's *This Morning* and Russell Brand's *Under the Skin* podcast, she has also been interviewed about dreaming by George Noory on Coast to Coast AM, Roman Kemp on Capital Radio, and on numerous other media outlets, including Today Extra, GMTV, Channel 4 and BBC Radio. She has given dream-decoding talks and webinars for leading companies and brands such as Beauty Bay, Anthropologie, Serge Lutens, Shiseido, Dusk Bedding, Immediate Media, the Mind Body Spirit Wellbeing festival, Conscious Life Expo and the Hearst Magazine group.

You can follow Theresa via her Facebook author pages and Instagram @thetheresacheung and learn more about her dreamwork at www.theresacheung.com.

'It may be that those who do most,
dream most.'

Stephen Butler Leacock